SALLY AND THE MAGIC RIVER

SALLY AND THE MAGIC RIVER

H. FRANK GAERTNER

AuthorHouse™ LLC
1663 Liberty Drive
Bloomington, IN 47403
www.authorhouse.com
Phone: 1-800-839-8640

Published by AuthorHouse 07/24/2014

ISBN: 978-1-4969-2681-4 (sc)
ISBN: 978-1-4969-2680-7 (e)

"Is all that we see or seem but a dream within a dream?"—Edgar Allan Poe, 1827

Chapter I

THE COINCIDENCE

The Hyundai Elantra looked like it had been in a demolition derby. Its jacked-up, deranged occupants had just robbed a Canejo Valley liquor store. The store's burglar alarm brought cops to the scene in time to see the getaway vehicle disappear into a nearby residential area. A cacophony of bullhorns, racing engines and squealing tires pursued the menace through a crosshatched neighborhood of caromed parked cars, flattened hedges and trenched yards. The police were about to trap the intruder when it bolted onto Lynn Road and headed west toward the Ventura-Freeway and an off-ramp crowded with biotechnologists on their workday morning commute from Agoura Hills and Westlake Village. And it's here, at this exit, where fate decided to have its way. Determined to escape, the disaster on wheels took the only way out, the wrong way.

Meanwhile, a mother and her ten-year-old daughter were traveling north from their home in Beverly Hills. The girl sat straining forward in the front seat of her family's classic Fleetwood-Brougham Cadillac anxiously anticipating a visit with her grandfather, a citrus rancher in the Santa Clara River Valley. Dad was away on business, so the two "women of the house" were on their own. The ten-year old was very fond of her grandfather, and enjoyed helping him in his workshop where he now spent most of his day making beautiful mahogany and ash C1 racing canoes. Such special moments with her grandfather and the solitude of the groves were the main things, but there was also one other thing, the enchanting and unpredictable Santa Clara River with its flood-plain sanctuary of rabbits, squirrels, coyotes, crows, and geese.

The mother knew her precocious daughter was more than ready to arrive at their intended destination. The child's upturned nose, imp-like smile, and bright green eyes made her look like a pixie imitating a race horse waiting for its starting gate to open. Earlier that morning she had wasted no time. She inhaled her breakfast, set her auburn hair in pigtails, and threw on a red checkered shirt, overalls, and hiking boots to certify that she was ready to "work" on the ranch as soon as they arrived. So, as fate would have it, the two travelers were buckled into the family's mega Cadillac by 7:30 am, and by 8:10 were entering that portion of the Ventura Freeway that passes through the city of Thousand Oaks.

Already scarred and now re-scarred by numerous glancing blows from its previous neighborhood chase and its reckless game of chicken up the off-ramp, the erratically driven wreck shot onto the freeway directly into the path of oncoming commuter traffic. Gaining speed to over ninety miles per hour, the motorists' worst nightmare crossed four lanes of traffic and, since miracles do happen, managed to reach the emergency shoulder adjoining the center divider. Seconds later, threading its way between oncoming traffic and the center divider, it successfully arrived at the freeway's next exit, the Moorpark Road underpass. But with its luck running out, "success" was to be short lived. As the Elantra crossed the underpass, a Toyota Celica, which had been attempting to avoid a rear end collision with the car ahead of it, spun out of control, only to be rear-ended itself by an eighteen-wheel Freightliner. The Toyota, partially airborne from the impact, continued its amazing thrill ride up and over the freeway guard-rail to the street below, where, in a Gallagher fantasy of gigantic proportions, it landed upright on a flatbed truck of watermelons where it began to head east, its new, unscheduled, direction. From Lynn Road to Moorpark Road, motorists, many in cars totaled from multiple collisions, sat unharmed. One would think every one of these fortunate, uninjured travelers would be giving thanks, simply grateful to be alive, but a few were way too busy fumbling with their dash-board mounted GoPro™ cameras to be so distracted.

At the same time the impacted big-rig, twisting violently, suddenly jackknifed across two lanes of traffic in a cloud of burning rubber and smoking brakes. With effective reaction times reduced to fractional seconds, a new group of hapless drivers began to form a chain of smashed fenders, damaged egos, and whiplash-injury lawsuits as Mercedes after BMW, after Jaguar found its mark on the luxury car of the wealthy biotechnology employee ahead of it.

The Elantra, having navigated four lanes of oncoming and a mile of narrow, center-divider emergency-lane, suddenly came into the Cadillac's view. And then, just as suddenly, it reacted to the out-of-control semi by hard-glancing the concrete retaining wall to meet head-on the Cadillac and its ranch-bound human cargo. The heavyweight car propelled itself forward, merging the Elantra's engine with front and rear seats and redirecting the motion of the compacted mass in the opposite, but now right, direction down the freeway. The collision launched both mother and daughter forward as if the two had been shot from guns. But, before their seat belts could carry the full burden of forward motion, the vintage Cadillac's newly retrofitted airbags exploded from their housings directly into the path of the would-be human projectiles. Traffic in both directions came to a complete stop as flying pieces of metal and glass made their way back to earth.

A surreal silence followed the mayhem. For some, the silence was interrupted by an appropriate heart-pounding, adrenaline-inflicted, involuntary, flight-response. For one, the silence momentarily intensified into a darkness more complete than any found in the deepest cavern.

Chapter II

THE JOURNEY BEGINS

"Wheeeee, this is great!" Sally shouted. As her ascent quickened, she could see the green beauty of the valley glide by between the clouds. "I've really got this down!" she said to herself. "I can't wait to show Mom and Dad. I wonder what they'll think when they see that I can fly? I just KNEW I could do it, and here I am actually flying wherever I want! Or at least wherever the wind wants," she corrected herself. A slight breeze, blowing her in the direction she wanted to go, had been masking the fact that she was not exactly in control.

Sally was five when her parents took her to see David Copperfield, the magician. Since then she had been trying to imagine herself stepping up and floating into the air, as she had seen him do, but it was stories by Richard Bach and her own recurring flying dreams that convinced her she could do it. Now it was actually happening!

"I'm going awfully high," she worried. "I wonder how high I will go?" The worry frightened her, because she could imagine herself drifting into space. Suddenly, her fear grew and she lost altitude. "Oh no!

I'm falling!" Her anxiety surged to the level of panic. "OHHHHHHEEEEEE," she screamed, losing it all together. Her descent gained momentum and sent her into a free-fall toward the Earth's surface. "I should've waited until I knew how to do this better!"

Her thoughts raced. "Why didn't I wait to show Mom and Dad? I should never have done this alone! If I had just stayed inside, I wouldn't have been able to go any higher than the ceiling. I knew I didn't know how to control this thing, but it was so much fun. PLEASE GOD, I DON'T WANT TO DIE!!! PLEASE HELP ME!!!" With the ground rushing to meet her, she somehow managed to feel at peace and relax. Her fear having dissipated, she rapidly decelerated, and landed, with a solid thunk, flat on her back, in a cushioning bed of wild flowers.

At first Sally didn't move. She just lay there watching clouds, she moments ago had visited, whisk by. "Good golly, that was close!" she said aloud to a passing butterfly. So many emotions filled her, but the fear was gone, and she was sooo glad to be alive. Everything was beautiful and safe again.

"What's up Sal? What'cha doin' layin' thar in dem flars like that?" quizzed Fidget, a very nervous hayseed version of a rabbit.

"Fidget! Fidget!!" Sally was really excited. "I flew! I flew!!" she repeated. "I actually took off and flew with those clouds up there!" At this remark, Fidget's nervous behavior increased, and he began to think Sally had gone completely off her rocker. "Sal," he said, "Ya know thar ain't no way ya could'a done that. Ya must'a had one'a dem dreams you bin habin' lately, whilst ya was layin thar."

"No, No Fidget." Sally became even more insistent and excited. "I flew, I flew." She was practically bursting with excitement. "I actually flew! I'd show you right now, but I need more practice. I have to be absolutely certain and unafraid that I can do it, or else I lose it. I almost killed myself just now!"

Fidget thought he'd best humor Sally for the time being, but as soon as he could get the rest of the gang together he intended to have the group help him talk some sense into her and bring her back to reality. "Wall den, ya jes shows me when ya gets ready. I shor wouldn't want'cha to go off an git yursef kilt, that's fer dang shor! Ya jes practice, an when ya git good at it, ya kin show me den."

Still excited, but calming down some, Sally said, "Oh, I will, I will, I will show you, and I will teach you how to do it too!"

Shuddering with nervous energy, the rabbit raised one eyebrow with a quizzical look, thinking that the best thing he could do now was just keep quiet.

Sally wanted to show Fidget this minute, but after that near death experience, she wasn't about to try flying again, at least not outdoors, and not until she had the matter entirely in her command. She thought, "I'll practice in my room, and graduate to taller buildings until I'm completely sure of myself. There's no way I can play it safe now by staying on the ground. It's way too much fun!"

The two friends began walking toward Sally's home on the other side of the valley. To her it was the most beautiful place in the world, and she was happy that Fidget had shown up to enjoy this wonderful day with her.

The valley was like a giant green bowl with splotches of flowers decorating its sides. Sally especially liked the wild mustard that cropped up in big yellow patches this time of year. The sky was already bright blue, but the penetrating whiteness of the alabaster clouds gave it an intense, super-realistic look. The tall grass lining the path waved and glistened with green iridescence. Sally could see her white, frame house in the distance, resting in the morning shade, slightly up the hill on the other side of the valley. There were oak, cottonwood, and willow trees around it, with a pond off to one side that had a solitary goose floating on its surface.

Of course there were other homes in Sally's valley, but she liked hers the best. The ranchers there grew walnuts, avocados, apricots, peaches, plums, figs, grapefruit, lemons, but mainly it was oranges. Many of the latter grew from older trees whose stature added shading and maturity to the beauty of the valley. Later these trees would be crowded with fruit bringing their shocking orange contrast to the green foliage, but at this time of year it was the amazing smell that made Sally feel as though she were in paradise. The trees were in bloom, and the valley was filled with citrus perfume.

The bees were enjoying this perfect day too. Each tree was covered with hundreds of them drawing nectar and gathering pollen from white blossoms. As the bees buzzed away in the morning air, they made it sound as if the entire valley were about to take off like an enormous airship. Sally delighted in sharing all this beauty with her long-eared companion. Her skip and whistle revealed her pleasure. As for Fidget, he was so proud to be Sally's friend he could not help but hop a little higher, and stand a little taller, whenever he was with her.

Sally thought, "Half the fun is going to be watching the surprised look on Fidget's face. I know he doesn't believe me." She was savoring this thought when flapping wings startled her, nearly touching her face.

Chapter III

AN OBSESSIVE IMAGE

S arah was a large, jet-black raven who never failed to find Sally when she was out walking. Although Sally was extremely pleased to see Sarah, Sally couldn't help but grimace a little in preparation for what she knew would happen next. Sarah's greeting included an air show, where she would soar high into the sky, caw three times, and dive to near ground level in a streak of black feathers that invariably scored a goal between Fidget's two, large, jack-rabbit ears. Today, Sarah offered no exception to her routine, and Fidget, as was his custom, pretended to be completely oblivious to the fact that his ears were now twisted around each other. The two friends always met in this fashion, and if their meeting were all that anyone saw, no one would think that they got along very well. However, upon further inspection, it was plain to see that their disdain was nothing but a playful act.

"Saleee," the raven called, as she zoomed straight up from the rabbit's ears-turned-goal-posts. She continued soaring into the sky and made a giant loop to dive once more and land atop a nearby orange tree.

Sally mused to herself; "I'll bet one day I'll fly like that." But she wasn't about to say anything to Sarah. The raven was a big tease, and would make fun of the idea until she saw for herself that Sally could do it. As for Fidget, Sally knew he wouldn't say anything. He was a good listener and kept things to himself.

When the two Earth-bound travelers caught up to Sarah, they were greeted with a question that left Fidget wondering more than just a little. "Saleee," the raven began in a crow accent that sounded like a cross between Steve Martin's Wild and Crazy Guy and Martin Short's Wedding Councilor. "How deed you geet wayee oveer heeer on thees side of ou'ware valeee zo airlee in zee marniing?"

Now <u>that</u> was a good question. Although Sally's home was visible on the opposing hill, she lived a good four miles away, and while Sally walked this way almost every weekend, it was a steady climb that took her at least an hour. She would have had to start walking by 6:30 to do it.

Sally stuttered, "I, I, I cccouldnt sleep."

That seemed to satisfy the raven, but Fidget knew Sally never got up that early on a weekend. The hour or so before seven was sacrosanct. It was her time for lying in bed to daydream about her canoe and the magic river. Sally's canoe was a one-of-a-kind, 15-foot, all wood, whitewater racer named Amber that was mounted on the west wall of the family's garage. The stunningly beautiful C-1 was made, raced, and on her sixth birthday, given to Sally by her Grandfather. Often, as she was heading off to

11

school with her Mom, they would get in the car, open the garage door, letting in the morning sunlight, and there would be Amber, her golden mahogany deck glowing, greeting Sally, beckoning.

When Sally was four she had seen a video of her Mom and Dad running their canoes through whitewater, and had ever since dreamed of the day that she herself would do it. Her Grandfather's gift had only heightened her desire. Sally spent many hours telling Fidget about this dream and how on weekends, before she got up in the morning, she would visualize herself paddling Amber through heavy rapids. She explained how after many months of such meditation the experience had become exceptionally vivid. She could see herself in heart-stopping detail guiding Amber through the entire course of the thunderous river. The image had become so real for her that she was sure that this magic river must exist, and, she told Fidget, *"Amber and I will someday run it."*

Fidget had a hard time understanding Sally's obsession with Amber and the river but he was sure Sally's father had something to do with it. Her father was a motivational speaker and Sally had picked up on and constantly repeated one of his sayings: "When you want something badly, imagine that it is here and now, right in front of you. The imagery will help you enjoy the process of getting what you want, and it will increase your chances of success."

It was evident to Fidget that Sally had followed her Dad's advice, and it had worked like a charm, because she now had the equivalent of a 3-D, video-game playing on her bedroom ceiling; one that got more real and more exciting every time she played it.

It was because of Sally's unwavering enthusiasm for this experience that Fidget knew she would not easily give it up, and it is why he began muttering to himself.

"How did she git here so early? What if'n she kin fly? Sal's neber lied ner tol' me make-believe stor'es bu'fore. Why wud she start now?" he continued to wonder. Fidget really began to fidget, his nervous nose practically wiggling off his face. "Wall she shor ain't goin' ta git <u>me</u> ta do it. That's fer <u>dang</u> shor!" He said the latter loud enough to bring a halt to Sally and Sarah's conversation about how delightful it was to be on this side of the valley in the morning. They both turned and looked at Fidget. Finally the raven broke the silence.

"Feegeet, who are you talkeeeng too? Are you seeiiing teeengs?" Sarah was always amused by Fidget, and <u>so</u> enjoyed getting his goat.

Totally flustered, Fidget tried to cover himself. "Ah sayid, it shor ain't goin ta rain. That's fer dang shor! That's what ah sayid, now leave me alone, Ah got me some powrful thankin' ta do."

Chapter IV

THE GANGS ALL HERE

Fortunately, Fidget had no time to think, it would have made him all the more fidgety. As it was, no one could think with the arrival of Gabby the gray squirrel. He was jumping all over the place and chattering a mile a minute. Rapidly, in one breath, not waiting for an answer, Gabby let loose with a string of questions.

"What are you all doing here so early? What's going on? Why wasn't I told about this? Is something important happening? Great morning, don't ya think? Anybody got any nuts? I'm famished. When are we going to eat?" Gabby continued his jabbering inquisition, "Where's Gandor and Carmine? Ya can't have a special meeting without them here. This is a special meeting isn't it? Why are we meeting so early anyway? We've never met this early in the morning before."

"Calm down, calm down Gabby," Sally said. "We're not having a special meeting. I just got up early."

When Sally was out for her Saturday morning expedition, Fidget, Sarah, Gabby, Carmine, and Gandor would eventually find Sally and have a meeting of sorts with her, usually while they ate lunch. The location of the meeting varied, but the agenda was always the same. Sally would go on about Amber and how she could not wait to experience the reality of taking Amber down her magic river. The animals would listen patiently, but with one exception, they could not understand her obsessive need to talk about the subject. That one exception was Gandor.

Gandor was the large goose who over-wintered on Sally's pond. He had found Sally's valley quite by accident when he was blown off course one year by a storm during his annual trek south to Mexico. Since that time he had always come back to this special place. He loved its beauty and solitude, and he liked the fact that the mad crush of thousands of noisy Canadian Honkers flying south didn't know about it. By the time summer was drawing to a close he had had quite enough of that raucous crowd. The winter months in this warm valley were just what he needed to calm his frayed nerves. Gandor never honked much himself, and just couldn't understand why the rest of his kind found it necessary to carry on so incessantly.

"I mean, it's enough to drive anyone to distraction," he had complained to Sally.

Gandor was wise, and so sensitive to things around him that he was, for all intents and purposes, clairvoyant. He listened to Sally talk about Amber and the river, and didn't think it the least bit strange that she was so single minded about it. On the contrary, during his last journey south from Canada, he experienced something so significant that it made him believe Sally would <u>have</u> to canoe the river with

Amber, or else she would be forced to face dangers even greater than those posed by powerful rapids. Strangely, as unnerving as the experience had been, Gandor was both excited and happy for Sally. His excitement made it hard for him not to tell everyone right away about his discovery, but he wanted to wait for just the right moment.

Gandor was proud of his ability to observe and see things that others could not see. That's why he was annoyed with himself when he woke to find Sally had somehow managed to slip past him. He was just getting ready for his morning-wake-up flapping ritual, when he heard her voice faintly in the distance. He lifted his long neck to get a better look, and trained his sharp eyes on the place where her voice seemed to originate. Although too far away to actually see and hear, his mind's eye perceived Sally talking to Fidget, Gabby, and Sarah.

"Most unusual," he thought. "How <u>did</u> she get way over there so early, and how <u>did</u> she do it without my knowing it?" Seriously puzzled, but not waiting a minute longer, not even to see if Sally left him any breakfast, he raised his giant wings, and with a single, wrenching beat, lifted himself off the surface of the pond.

A short time later, on the other side of the valley, Gabby was continuing to talk about nothing in particular, and everything in general, and had all but split a verbal gasket when Gandor gracefully settled down next to him, giving Gabby quite a start.

"Gandy," Gabby said in his shrill voice. "We were just talking about you! Where's Carmine? When are we going to start the meeting! Isn't this great? We're meeting for breakfast! We've never done that before, you know. What'd you bring for us to eat! I'm so hungry I could eat a walnut, shell and all!"

"Ya got a one track mind Gabby," admonished Fidget. "That's fer dang shor! Alls'ya ben talkin' about dis marnin' is feedin' yer face," said Fidget. "All right den," he continued, "Ah might as well go git us some'a dem cair'ts ober der." Fidget hopped off toward a small field of carrots that Farmer Martin had planted near his home.

Sally called, "Wait up Fidget, I'll go with you to see if we can't get one of Mrs. Martin's apple pies for breakfast. Good to see you Gandor!" Sally greeted Gandor in passing with a big grin on her face. "I'm glad you could make it!" she teased. The large brownish gray and white goose could see that Sally was rather pleased with herself for having successfully slipped by him earlier. "I'll see if Mrs. Martin has some of her corn bread too!"

After that last comment from Sally, the embarrassment that was beginning to ruffle Gandor's feathers left him, and he almost forgot himself by releasing a very undignified and un-Gandor-like honk. He held back however, and began to savor the thought of Mrs. Martin's corn bread, which was his favorite thing to eat.

"Did you see Carmine on your flight over here?" asked Sally. "Carmine really likes Mrs. Martin's corn bread and pies too."

As it happens, Gandor <u>had</u> seen Carmine, and had let her know that they were about to have an early morning meeting.

"Yes, said Gandor, I told her to come over to the Martin's place. She should be here any minute."

No sooner had Gandor finished saying it, than Carmine came running up. Carmine was a good-looking and swift coyote. She was especially quick today, because Gandor's call to her had let her know that something very special was up. Carmine had come to the valley with her Mom. They had left their home in Mexico when Carmine was still a baby. Her Dad had been killed by a mountain lion, and her Mom had jumped with Carmine held safely in her mouth into a boxcar hitched to a slowly moving freight train, narrowly escaping the lion's attack themselves. When they reached the border they crossed it on foot and made the rest of the two-day journey in the back of a van that happened to stop in Sally's valley. Tired and hungry they began to look for food, but their search developed an unusual complication. Her Mom must have felt the fear and pain of the lion's attack, because she could not bring herself to eat meat or kill another animal again. So it came to pass that Carmine was raised on vegetables, fruits, and nuts, and on the milk and eggs that farmer Martin left for them.

Farmer Martin had seen the mother coyote and her pup soon after they had arrived in the valley from Mexico. The two were just sitting there staring up at him from the front of the ranch house. They looked extremely hungry and he could tell by the mother coyote's shaggy coat that she really needed a nutritious meal. The mother and pup were not bothering his chickens, so he decided to see if he could keep the coyotes happy by feeding them milk and eggs. Every morning he placed milk with raw eggs mixed in under the willow tree beside the ranch house, and watched proudly as the mother coyote grew stronger and healthier, and as Carmine grew into a beautiful young lady. He had once considered getting a dog to watch over his chickens and the ranch, but these two turned out to be very protective of the Martin's farm, so there was no need for a dog after their arrival.

Chapter V

PASTORAL PLEASANTRIES

M rs. Martin was as fond of the coyotes as was Mr. Martin, and she was also very partial to Sally and the other animal characters in the cadre. It was only natural then, when she saw Sally, Fidget, Gandor, Carmine, Gabby, and Sarah coming her way, she knew just what they wanted, and hurried off to her pantry to get it. She was surprised to see them so early. She had not seen Sally and her friends before noon on any other Saturday, and she was wondering what was so special about today. No matter, she had already prepared Sally's favorite peanut butter and mayonnaise sandwich, a combination that, surprisingly, she happened to like herself, and she added Gandor's favorite corn bread, along with some apples, plums, grapes, peaches, and walnuts, the latter primarily destined for consumption by you know who. She placed it all, along with a thermos of milk and a red checkered blanket that matched Sally's shirt, into a basket she herself had woven.

Mrs. Martin had just finished baking four apple pies, so her home was filled with the wonderful smell of apples, nutmeg, and cinnamon. She placed a warm pie on top of the blanket and closed the basket. She didn't bother including carrots because she knew that Fidget enjoyed getting the carrots himself. And, by the time that she finished assembling the goodies and eating utensils for Sally's use, the excited and somewhat unruly troop arrived at Mrs. Martin's doorstep.

"Why Sally, it's so good to see you and your friends this morning," enthused Mrs. Martin. It never failed to brighten her day to see Sally with her menagerie. There was Gandor strutting proudly by Sally's side, Carmine pacing nervously in the background licking her chops, Sarah diving back and forth in anticipation of all the delicious morsels she was about to retrieve, Gabby chattering away at Sally's feet about who knows what, and in the distance, Fidget, doing what all rabbits like to do best in a field of carrots.

"How did you get here so early?" Mrs. Martin asked. "Did you fly?"

In response to Mrs. Martin's facetious question Sally just smiled brightly and said, "Yes Mam," knowing full well that Mrs. Martin would not believe her "yes" answer, and would just think she herself was being funny.

"Well, you must have gotten up awfully early to get here by this time. I prepared a nice lunch for you, but I bet you wouldn't mind having it for breakfast would you?" Mrs. Martin asked, knowing ahead of time what Sally's answer would be.

"No Mam, we wouldn't mind at all! Would we?" asked Sally, turning to her friends, who were obviously becoming impatient with the human banter. "That would be great!" Sally added. "As you can see, we are all starved to death after our morning walk." Feeling more talkative than usual, Sally continued, "It is really nice being over here on this side of the valley in the morning. The sun comes up a lot earlier over here. Our house is still in the shade of the hillside. I'm sure I will be coming here at this time more often, now that I know how nice it is. It's cooler, and seems a lot fresher and shinier than it does at noon. It must be the dew that makes it sparkle so."

Sally could have enthused on and on, she was so pleased to be here, especially given her new method of travel. However, Mrs. Martin interrupted her saying. "Well, anytime you and your friends want to come for breakfast instead of lunch is just fine with me. If you will just let me know ahead of time, I will have a more appropriate breakfast ready for you."

"Oh no," said Sally, "The lunch you fix for us is just perfect." Sally was thinking about the peanut butter and mayonnaise sandwich and how her Mom always insisted that she eat her oats in the morning. A peanut butter and mayonnaise sandwich for breakfast would be a <u>real</u> treat!

"Well then, here is your basket," Mrs. Martin said. "Be careful now. I've placed the apple pie on top. Keep the basket straight so that you don't spill the pie all over the blanket."

"Oh I will be careful," said Sally. "Thank you so much, Mrs. Martin!" Sally accepted Mrs. Martin's basket without embarrassment as bartering goods and services was the way most business was done in the valley. Sally's family and the Martins traded favors regularly. "You are the best!" beamed Sally with an ear to ear grin. Mrs. Martin returned Sally's smile with one of her own. Waving goodbye, and glad to be alive on such a perfect day, Sally and her followers headed toward a grassy hill by a willow tree near the Martin's house, where they could eat lunch, have their meeting, and command a sweeping view of the valley below.

Carmine, who had hung back, quietly observing all of the proceedings since her arrival, finally spoke up. "Muy bien! Vamanos a comer!" Carmine said with a fake heavy accent. She really didn't know all that much Spanish but would throw some in every now and then just for emphasis and to remind everyone of her Mexican heritage. "I hope Mrs. Martin gave us plenty of corn bread," she added, now with almost no accent at all. "That's my favorite!"

There was always plenty of corn bread, but nevertheless, it made Gandor very nervous for Carmine to talk like that. His bill had been watering for that bread ever since Sally had suggested it, and he wasn't about to let Carmine have more than her fair share.

"There's plenty enough for everyone." Sally announced, feeling the tension mounting as they all anticipated having breakfast at last.

Sally opened the basket, took out the blanket, and spread it on the grassy slope of the little hill. Carmine paced back and forth behind Sally, salivating with her tongue hanging out. Gandor parked himself directly in front of the basket in as dignified a manner as he could under the

circumstances. All the stress he was experiencing waiting
for the food made Gandor's tail feathers nervously flutter,
and caused his head to bob back and forth in the direction
of the open basket. Gabby was the worst of the bunch. He
couldn't sit still nor could he stop chattering. He wagged
his bushy tail at Sally like someone incessantly pushing
a button on an elevator trying to make it move faster.
Sarah was the only one of Sally's troop who showed any
manners at this moment. However, Sarah was just biding
her time. Her mannerly behavior would be short lived,
as her favorite sport was to dive-bomb the picnickers
while they were eating, often picking off an unsuspecting
diner's next bite. And of course, there was Fidget. He was
just now returning from the carrot patch.

Fidget always went to the carrot patch with good
intentions, planning to bring back carrots for everyone.
However, no matter how good his intentions, all the
carrots he pulled up got eaten before he could ever get to
the picnic. Although he would eat a lot of carrots on the
spot, he would invariably leave the patch hopping away
with a few carrots in his mouth to share, but alas, the
temptations along the way never failed to be too much for
him. He would have to stop to rest a little and munch a
little, so that by the time he was back with everyone, the
carrots were gone and he was quite full. Today was no
exception. "Ah ate all mah cair'ts," Fidget said, with more
than just a little embarrassment. "Ah guess Ah'l hafta go
get some more after Ah rest up some."

"That's okay Fidget," Sally assured him, as she began
to pass out the food to the others. "We have more than
enough to eat."

It was as though Sally had a magic wand. As soon as she began to pass out the food, everyone's character abruptly changed. The anxiety left, and the chatter stopped, as did the nervous fluttering, bobbing, jumping, and pacing. It would have gotten absolutely quiet were it not for the sounds of smacking mouths, clicking beaks, clacking bills, and cracking nuts. Sally savored her peanut butter and mayonnaise sandwich and planned to leave plenty of room for the apple pie. The apples, plums, peaches and grapes too were enjoyed by all, with the exception of Fidget who was already stuffed.

Fidget was about to nod off when Gandor spoke in a voice loud enough for everyone to hear and intense enough that Fidget jumped, opened his eyes wide, and hopped forward to get a better listening post. Gandor's commanding voice also caught Sarah in mid dive, as she was about to swipe some corn bread right from under Carmine's nose. She instead fluttered down to the blanket to listen to Gandor herself. Gandor didn't speak often, but when he did it tended to be very interesting, especially his predictions of the future.

Chapter VI

THE DISCLOSURE

"Sally," Gandor said in his most authoritative voice. "I have discovered something very important; something that I believe will affect each one of us, including myself, in a most significant way."

At that comment everyone froze in place and held their breath. Gandor's solemn tone and formal demeanor meant what he had to say was most serious.

"We have been listening for many weeks to Sally speak of Amber and a mysterious river that she 'sees' in her morning meditations. Although we've patiently listened to her, none of us have been able to understand her obsession with it. Until recently, I was satisfied, as you have been, that her river was just a fantasy, and that her canoe adventure was nothing more than lunchtime conversation. But after what I've experienced, I believe her river is real, and that she will be compelled to do what she has been describing. In fact, I am now certain that accepting the challenge will prove to be unavoidable. I do not understand why this is so, nor am I clear what role the rest of us will play. However, I <u>do</u> know that, when the time comes, each one of us will somehow be there to help."

Carmine paced furiously. Gabby had grown uncharacteristically silent, and his tail swished in a way that signaled his intense concern. Fidget invented a new meaning to the word fidget. His nose flared and wiggled at the same time his mouth moved up and down in an agitated way like a chipmunk's. To emphasize his anxiety his right hind leg began a rapid-fire thumping motion. Sarah resumed her acrobatic flight but quickly brought it to a halt by landing on Sally's shoulder. The raven wanted Sally to know that she was not going to be abandoned by her friends, no matter what.

Gandor continued, "During my flight south from Canada this year I passed over one of the rivers that courses through the High Sierras. This one had endless rapids, enormous waves, deep holes, massive rocks, cascades, and waterfalls, but that is not what caught my attention. I felt watched, and, as I flew over the river, I heard a deep, booming voice that seemed to come from the river itself, saying *'Tell Sally I am waiting for her. I have a secret that she alone must know.'*"

As if on cue, a solitary, black cloud moved into position directly above the picnickers. The effect punctuated Gandor's words, blanketing the valley in ominous, darkened tones, much as a total eclipse of the sun might do.

Gandor continued: "Needless to say, I was frightened by the voice, but, even so, I did not immediately leave, hoping I could learn more. Although the voice did not speak again, I flew away from that place certain that Sally's very <u>life</u> would depend on her canoeing that river to learn its secret."

Now the silence was complete. Even the birds stopped chirping and the bees stopped buzzing. It was as though time itself had come to a standstill.

"Oh my!" Gabby was first to break the silence and express his great alarm with a voice nearly rising to glass-shattering decibels. "How can we possibly help?"

"Y'y'y'ya," stuttered Fidget, "A,A,Ah'm jist a rabbit. How ahm Ah goin' ta git to the High Saharas, er whatevah they're called, much less do anythin' useful on a ragin' wildt river?" he pondered out loud.

"Well I can get to those mountains," Carmine boasted. "If my Mom and I can come all the way from Mexico, I'm sure I can make it to Sally's river." Carmine was still worriedly pacing, as it was her canine custom to do, but she was brave, and would unquestioningly help Sally any way she could.

In the midst of all this commotion, Sally sat calmly with a big smile on her face. She knew that Gandor spoke the truth, and it was a relief to know that there was, after all, great importance to her recurring, increasingly realistic, vision of the river and her single-minded determination for her and Amber to run it. She was intrigued by Gandor's insistence that he and the others would help, and was both amused and disturbed by the impossible mental picture of a rabbit, coyote, raven, squirrel, and goose riding on

Amber's deck through dangerous whitewater. "How can they help me, and how can they possibly survive such a journey?" she wondered.

This last thought worried Sally. However, before she got too concerned, Gandor's calming voice interrupted her thoughts.

"Sally, I know that it is difficult for you to understand how we can help you. I don't understand that myself. Nevertheless, we <u>will</u> help you, and we <u>will</u> come through this great adventure safely. You just have to believe, accept and trust in the outcome. Do not worry about the future. Worry accomplishes nothing anyway. Just enjoy each moment, know that all is well, and that you will acquire the skill and capability necessary to handle the next thing to come your way. Fear is your worst enemy. In truth it is your only enemy. Release your fear and you can accomplish anything. I believe this is an important lesson the river has to teach, and it is a lesson that each one of us can learn. However, it is not the secret the river holds for you Sally. That secret <u>is</u> beyond my knowing. You and Amber alone must unlock its meaning."

"Th'thank you Gandor, you have helped me understand the significance of my magic river." Sally was both elated and worried. She would have to learn to face fear with grace and poise, to be confident in the face of dangers she could not imagine. Her mind raced, filling her with conflict. Excitement, fear, wonder, awe, amazement; it was almost more than her short ten years of life could bear, but the mental turmoil abruptly ended with a certainty of what she must do next. The others were confused, and one, a still-trembling rabbit, had been terrified by Gandor's words. But she would show them how she could get to the river. And she would let them see firsthand the magic powers that had already begun to assemble in their corner of the universe.

"I'll put their minds at ease," she thought, reassuring herself.

Sarah, who had maintained her perch on Sally's shoulder, said, "Aheee for one am redee to help where evair Saleee needs mae."

"M'M" Me t't'too, stuttered Gabby.

"And of course you already know that you can count on me," followed Carmine.

"Ah shor don't know how ah kin be of any help, but Ah'l do mah best," said the rabbit in his most unsteady and slowest drawl yet. "Maybe ah kin brang some cair'ts." he ended weakly.

"You'll do great!" Sally spoke with newfound authority. "I know you will. I don't know the river's secret, nor do I know yet how I will ever figure it out, but I do have a secret of my own to show you!"

Chapter VII

SHOWING OFF

"I wasn't going to do this again until I was safely indoors, but with your help I think I can do it without much risk." Sally's voice was hesitant, but a calculating smile and determined nod reestablished her conviction.

Fidget began whacking his right hind leg furiously against the blanket. His ears stood straight up and he got a wild look in his eyes, which now were intermittently crossing at the same time his nose, whiskers, and buck front-teeth jockeyed for position on his face. He was the only one among Sally's friends who had any idea what was about to happen, and the more he thought about it the more agitated he became.

Gandor was perplexed. Taken off-guard by Sally's actions for the second time in one day, he rocked back and forth, shifting his weight from one foot to the other. "What is she up to?" he wondered.

With a serious tone, Sally continued. "All right everybody, pay close attention, here is what I want you to do." She was mysterious on purpose. The expectation of witnessing the surprise that would soon sweep over her audience was approaching a feeling close to an adult's version of ecstasy. She wondered why the idea of surprising her friends should be so delicious. Maybe it was her own liking of surprises, or maybe it was her mischievous personality. No matter, she <u>was</u> going to surprise them, and she was going to enjoy every minute of it.

"I'm going to lie down on my back on the blanket with my arms and legs extended away from my body." Sally instructed, "Carmine, I want you to grab hold of my right pant leg with your teeth. Gandor, I would like you to hang on tight with your bill to my other leg. Gabby, you can take hold of my right shirt-sleeve near the wrist, and Fidget you can hold my other sleeve. Sarah, you, please, stand on my stomach and supervise."

"What are you going to do Sally?" Gabby was getting worried himself. "Why do you want us to do that? Are you going to fly off the ground or something?" he joked, not knowing how close he was to the truth. "How's our doing this going to help us understand anything? Can't you give us a clue? I'm going to feel pretty silly with your shirt in my mouth."

He said all this in one excited breath, but before he could say anything more, Gandor said, "Do as Sally says, and just watch." Finally, Gandor was getting a mental picture of the coming events, and he was getting as tickled as Sally. He liked surprises too, and always enjoyed watching the expressions on his listeners' faces when he forecast their future. "This is going to be a <u>splendid</u> surprise!" he said to himself, anticipating what was about to happen.

Carmine interrupted Gandor's thoughts with, "Si, si, vamanos a ver que pasa! Let's see what happens!" once again using a thick Spanish accent because she thought something important was about to happen. "Pienso que esto sera <u>muy</u> bueno."

Fidget was a basket case by now. His slow speech contrasted strangely with his agitated body movements. "Ah know whaats goin' to happen, and Ah don't like it one bit. Ah'll hold on, but it jist ain't right. Ah'm only a rabbit and Ah've had about all the excitement Ah kin take fer one day!" Fidget was telling the truth; he was thoroughly exhausted from all the nervous energy he had expended.

"Zo, yew jeest want mae to stand up haer and direct everyteeng?" Sarah was really puzzled. "How can Ahee do they't whean Ahee don' know wat Ahee'm supposed to dew?"

"Jeest yew watch mae. You veel know whaat to dew." Sally light-heartedly imitated Sarah as a way to relieve some of the mounting tension. "Okay now. Is everyone in position? Does everyone have a good hold?" she asked.

"Ye'ff," barked Carmine through her teeth.

Sarah, the only one of Sally's attendees whose mouth was not full, called out her first on- board report, "Ayveree wan ees raydee. Whaat hoppeens nayxt?"

"Just hang on!" Sally answered, already concentrating her thoughts. "This may take a few minutes." She began to repeat quietly "I <u>can</u> do it. I <u>release</u> all fear. I <u>can</u> do it. I <u>release</u> all fear. I <u>can</u> do it. I <u>release</u> all fear."

When Sally repeated the chant, Carmine, Gabby, and Sarah looked at each other in bewilderment, and then in unison turned to look at Sally, as if she were possessed. Gandor, on the other hand, having had a premonition of what was about to happen, planted his webbed feet firmly on the ground and tightened his bill on Sally's pant leg. As for Fidget, a strange peace had come over him. It was as though he'd overloaded his circuits and blown a fuse. He sat there with Sally's sleeve in his mouth, with a blank look and a silly rabbit's grin on his face.

Over and over, Sally chanted the phrase "I <u>can</u> do it. I <u>release</u> all fear" until she began to slowly lift off the blanket. As she rose higher, she continued chanting, but now with more affirmation, intensity and speed, "I <u>am</u> doing it! I <u>release</u> all fear! I <u>am</u> doing it! I <u>release</u> all fear," and then louder and louder until she was almost shouting. "I <u>am</u> doing it. I release <u>all</u> fear!!"

Sally was nearly three feet off the ground. Fidget and Gabby were already swinging in the space below Sally's arms, whereas Gandor and Carmine stretched downward to maintain their contact with the ground while each retained a grip on one of Sally's pant legs.

"Felp!" muffled Fidget, suddenly breaking out of his trance. "Geh 'ee 'own, geh 'ee 'own!!" If you are a rabbit hanging in the air with a sleeve in your mouth, "Get me down!" can be a very hard thing to say.

Chapter VIII

UNEXPECTED RESULTS

T he human airship, with Sarah at the helm, continued its ascent.

"Salee," Sarah cawed, "Ahee theenk yew betair gait us down. Fidgeet ees about to fall!"

Fidget was kicking wildly, trying to climb the air, and hanging on for dear life to Sally's shirt. Sally was ten feet off the ground and rising. She knew that if she didn't do something they would continue to rise, and that would put Fidget, Carmine, and Gabby in grave danger. This had not worked out as expected. She never imagined she would be able to carry everyone with her. It was as if there were steel cables attached to sky-hooks pulling her skyward. She had to do something quick, but what? A big dose of fear now would send her falling to the ground with the distinct possibility that she would fall on top of Fidget, Gabby, Carmine, or Gandor, who were still dangling from her shirt sleeves and pant legs. She needed some way to induce just the right amount of anxiety, not too much and not too little, to lower herself to the ground gently.

"I need a fear-rheostat." The strange thought only added confusion to Sally's racing mind. "What a mess I'm in. I knew better than to do this, but I couldn't resist showing everybody! When will I ever learn?" Sally shouted, "Fidget, Gabby, hang on! Don't worry, I will get us down safely." She was far from confident about the last declaration, but she was going to do everything in her power to make it come true. She quickly judged the distance to the ground and abruptly took action by calling out, "Let go, Carmine!"

In response to Sally's order to Carmine, Gandor released his grip and began flying beside Sally. "Let go, Carmine," he repeated. "You only have a short distance to fall. I can stay here with Sally, and I <u>think</u> I know how to help her."

"Okay," Carmine barked, as she trustingly released herself from Sally's leg and fell, landing hard but safely a short distance from the blanket.

When Gandor and Carmine released their grip, Sally tipped slightly, righted herself without knowing how she did it, and continued to rise more rapidly; fifty feet, one hundred feet, two hundred feet: higher and faster she climbed.

Gabby scrambled up Sally's arm and moved over to Sally's chest, close to where Sarah was perched. "What are we going to do now?" Gabby asked. How are you going to get us out of this one Gandor? What's the ---?"

Before Gabby could finish his last question, there was a shrill cry for help, and a screech of "Feeegeeet!!!" from Sarah that sounded more like a hawk than a crow. In his attempt to join Gabby and Sarah on Sally's topside, Fidget lost his grip on Sally's shirt, and was plummeting to the ground, which was now almost five hundred feet below. The rabbit's surprisingly professional-looking skydive was rudely, but thankfully, interrupted. Just in time, Gandor snagged Fidget by his tail, and then gently deposited him on the picnic blanket. Having done this in one swooping motion, Gandor quickly returned to his job of assisting the rapidly ascending dirigible named Sally.

Fidget lay panting, rigid with fright after his unrehearsed free-fall. His legs stood straight up, very un-rabbit like, as he and Carmine watched the sky-show unfold above them.

When Gandor reached Sally's side he instructed Sarah to abandon ship and join him in flight. "What about Gabbee?" she said.

"I will take care of Gabby," Gandor responded. "Gabby, let me fly you down to Fidget and Carmine. Sarah and I will help Sally get back safely."

"Oh no you don't. I'm staying right here with Sally," Gabby insisted. "Maybe I can help. Anyway, I can hang on to Sally with no difficulty and I can move to any position on her if I need to. I've always wanted to fly. As you know some of my cousins are <u>great</u> fliers."

"All right, but you are on your own," said Gandor. "I don't have time to argue with you. I'm going to ask Sally to roll over, and I want you to move to her back as she is doing it."

"No problem," Gabby replied confidently. "It will be a piece of cake!"

Sarah took off saying, "Saleee, Gandor, and Ahee veel guide you down."

"OK, here we go!" Sally exclaimed. "Move with me Gabby, and please don't fall off!"

"Don't worry Sally! You forget! I'm a *squirrel*!!"

Chapter IX

A WEIGHTY PROBLEM

S ally rolled over and saw Carmine and Fidget on the blanket below. They appeared to be shrinking in size as she continued to rise to more than one thousand feet. Gabby quickly scrambled to a new place on Sally's back.

"Ok, Sally, it's time for you to show your stuff," Gandor said with calm confidence.

"But Gandor," Sally objected, "I don't know how to control my altitude, my speed, or my direction."

"Don't worry, Sally." Gandor assured her. "I've been thinking about that, and I believe I know a method you can use. Listen to me carefully." Gandor began a lengthy lecture, while the group continued to drift upward. "You first had to believe with all your heart, mind, and soul that you could fly. You then had to free yourself of all fear. You now have those matters under your command. You know you can fly, because you are right this minute doing it, and you know that if you become afraid, you will fall. Therefore, you know without question that you can have no room for fear. It is a simple matter of life or death for you. Release your fear and you will soar. Become fearful, and you will fall. These are very simple, but <u>very</u> uncompromising facts. That is why I am sure you will never be able to use fear to get yourself safely down, but I believe there <u>is</u> a way."

Sally and Sarah were listening intently to Gandor, as they continued to glide higher, approaching the clouds and the two thousand-foot mark.

"Just as your fearlessness and imagination have made you lighter than air, I think you should be able to use your imagination to make yourself as heavy as you want. For example you can picture yourself with weights on your hands and feet. Let's say three pounds each at first." Gandor paused for a moment letting what he just said sink in. Then he continued: "Go ahead, Sally. Go ahead and try it."

Sally immediately saw, in her mind's eye, weights of three pounds each in her hands and attached to her feet. Her ascent slowed, stopped, and she started to fall, slowly at first and then steadily faster. The wind rushed by, as she took the stable pose of a skydiver in free-fall, the same pose she had seen watching videos of her Dad's jumps. She traveled a few hundred yards this way, then mentally discarded the weight in her right hand in an effort to slow down. This act seriously affected her balance and almost sent her spinning. She mentally discarded the remaining weights only to be caught by the opposing wind, which blew her like a feather straight up. Just as she was about to tumble out of control, she rebalanced herself by adding and subtracting weights, first on one side and then the other, back and forth until she stabilized and rid herself of all the weights.

"Whew!" Sally sighed, exhausted from the mental effort and physical exertion. "That was a close!" Gandor had the right idea, but his attached-weight method was way too clumsy. Gandor and Sarah were catching up to Sally, and she was about to turn to them for help when she remembered the "fear-rheostat." Her Mom had explained the principle of the rheostat to her when she installed a dimmer switch for the light in the chandelier over the family's dining room table. Sally liked the idea of having the fine control that a rheostat could bring, but Gandor was right, a fear-based one wouldn't do. It would be impossible for her to imagine a continuous scale of fear. "What <u>does</u> a little more fear look like anyway?" she asked herself.

But weight was different. It was easy to imagine how additional weight would look and feel. A weight-rheostat tied to her left wrist was not at all difficult to imagine. She could see herself dialing a little knob and adjusting her weight up or down from zero to her earth-bound weight of 65 pounds. At an imagined weight of zero her lack of fear and complete faith that she could fly would leave her lighter than air as she was now. At 65 pounds she would fall just as any person would. Somewhere between 0 and 65 she would be able to achieve the ideal surface to weight ratio for human flight.

Sally was back to more than 2000 feet when, without a word to Gandor and Sarah, who were now flying beside her, she tried falling once more. This time she imagined using the rheostat dial to increase her weight from zero to what she thought <u>might</u> be a good diving-weight, about 25 pounds. Her ascent slowed, then stopped, and she began falling at a slight forward angle to the ground. The speed of her downward and forward motion increased rapidly. She sped toward the earth, accelerating as the law of gravity demanded. She then slowly adjusted her imaginary rheostat until her fall slowed, and began to rise, but this time she maintained some forward momentum.

A triumphant realization spread across her face. She had discovered how to increase her air-speed and control her forward motion, and she had done it on her own! Much as birds gain speed and momentum when they dive, Sally found she could gain all the speed she wanted with a diving maneuver, and she could move laterally just by adjusting the angle of descent with her body. Also, since she could change her weight continuously, with practice she would be able to find the perfect adjustment of her rheostat. Soon she would be able to sail and glide on thermal updrafts just as she had seen Gandor and Sarah do. For now, she decided simply to enjoy the thrill of diving and soaring as her means of travel. She would eventually lose altitude, but whenever she lost too much she could always dial her weight to zero and rise like a hot air balloon.

Gandor and Sarah finally caught up to Sally and were gliding beside her. She shouted to them, "Wow, this is even more fun than my earlier flight! This morning I just floated wherever the wind blew me. I had no control of my direction or speed. Now I really <u>can</u> fly wherever <u>I</u> want!"

"Saleee," Sarah called above the sound of the rushing wind. "Yew veel make a vonderfel baird! Vee can fly togaethair!"

Gandor was so elated he literally honked with joy, "Go for it Sally! Show us what you can do!"

Sally was totally unafraid of heights or of falling now. Even at 2000 feet and nothing below her but thin air, she was filled with confidence, and believed she was perfectly safe in this new environment. "However," she thought. "I will want to wear warmer clothes. It's really chilly up here."

Sally pulled her arms to her side, imagined adjusting the rheostat to read her earth-bound weight, and headed into a steep dive rapidly approaching a speed of 60 miles per hour. Quickly, and with much less effort than before, she mentally began to lighten her load by adjusting the imaginary dial on her left wrist with her right hand, and moved her arms to point directly in front of her, Superman style. With this motion, and the mental gymnastics needed for weight adjustment, she thrust herself upward into an exhilarating roller-coaster-like climb.

Suddenly, Sally heard a loud shrill voice directly behind her right ear, "Yowee! Go! Go! Go! What a ride! Do it again! More! More! Give me more!" Sally had forgotten all about Gabby hanging on to the back of her overalls, who, until that moment, had been rendered speechless for the first time in his life.

Surprised, Sally turned her head toward the voice and tried to shout above the wind that was now screaming by her face. "Are you all right, Gabby?" Sally's auburn pigtails extended like rigid rods on either side of the wild-eyed squirrel.

"Yes, Yes," he shouted back. "Do it again! Do it again!" Gabby was always excited, but he was <u>way</u> beyond that now. An amusing thought occurred to Sally, who was a little pleased herself, to say the least. She giggled into the wind, "Maybe Gabby and I were birds in a previous life."

"Okay Gabby," she finally replied, "but we will have to do it later. I'm getting cold."

Yet again Gandor and Sarah caught up to the amazing duo. Drawing to a glide beside Sally, Gandor exclaimed excitedly, "I thought it was going to take <u>weeks</u> for you to learn how to control your flight. How did you do that?"

Sally explained to Gandor how she had altered his method of adding and subtracting weights from her feet and hands. Gandor was impressed that she was able to come up with this innovation so quickly. Her method of adjusting a rheostat to alter the weight of an airborne object, especially since the object was her own body, was unique in the annals of flying history. No bird or man-made flying machine had ever flown the way Sally was doing it. She had combined the aerodynamic attributes of a skydiver with those of a lighter-than-air ship. Gandor realized that she would be able to do things in the air that no one, including birds, had ever done.

It would take Sally some time to learn all of her new capabilities, but for now she had a diving, gliding flight-plan that she thought would work well enough. She was anxious to try some of the new maneuvers that she had in mind, but now it was more important to get back to the picnic blanket. Sally was still worried about Fidget. She was pretty sure that he was OK, but she was sorry that she had given him such a fright. She only wanted to surprise him, not scare him to death! She was learning that surprises weren't always welcome. Moreover, Sally could tell from all of the pacing that Carmine was doing that the coyote was more than a little anxious to have this sky-show come to a close.

Sally mused out loud, "I'm really getting cold! I must get down and see that Fidget is okay. If it wasn't for Gandor ---." Sally's words trailed off as she began to think the unthinkable. "Are you ready Gabby?" she shouted, as much to interrupt her own scary thoughts as to notify the squirrel of her impending dive.

"You know I am," Gabby squealed in his highest voice yet. "Let's dive all the way to the blanket!" he added bravely.

"All right den," Sally said, feeling great and playfully mimicking Fidget's low, rabbit voice. "You asked for it Gabby! Hang on tight!" she warned.

"Be careful!" an alarmed Gandor cautioned. "You don't know everything you need to know yet! Watch out for that thermal ahead of you!" But before the last words could reach her, Sally was gone, rapidly descending into her most daring free-fall yet.

"Saleee!!" Sarah screeched. "Wait!" Then Sarah did something that no raven or crow had ever done. She tucked in her wings, streamlined her body like a hawk, and followed Sally in a fearless, head long dive. Sally had heard Sarah's screech, and had turned to see Sarah following her, but was too far away to notice the look of alarm in Sarah's eyes.

Chapter X

PILOT ERROR

S ally followed a steep glide path, rapidly approaching one hundred miles per hour. She fell through a thousand feet of air space before a strong uplift, created by a Santa Ana blowing against a westward cliff, tossed her back up the way she had come. Rebounding, as if from a giant trampoline, Sally flailed out of control like a rag-doll trapped in a game of pitch and toss.

"Help!" Sally cried, realizing that she had once more gotten herself into trouble. "When <u>will</u> I stop letting my enthusiasm get the best of me? Hang on Gabby! Are you still there?" she asked with urgency. The column of air was no longer supporting her. She had come to the apogee of her wild ride on the thermal elevator.

"Yes," Gabby replied weakly. They were already beginning to fall back to earth. He had just experienced the ride of his life, more than he had ever bargained for, and he wanted to get off. 'Off,' unfortunately, was not an option. The ride was far from over.

Sally, disoriented by the preceding violent tumble, was unable to take the stable sky-diver's position. Instead, she began flipping end-over-end. Quickly, she mentally dialed her wrist rheostat, reducing her imagined weight to zero. **But nothing happened! Her fall continued to accelerate!** The stress of the flipping motion forced her to draw her body into a ball that sent her spinning head-first like a high-diver doing a summersault-dive into a swimming pool more than a thousand feet below. She tried the rheostat, again, and again, with no success!

"Oh Gabby," she thought. "Please <u>hang on</u>!" She dared not think what was happening to him. "I'm so afraid for ---!" and then she got it! "I'm frightened!! No wonder I'm falling! No wonder the rheostat hasn't been working!"

Falling and spinning at more than one hundred miles per hour, she let go of her fear. She stopped trying to control her fall. She just let it happen. She saw herself and her friends as happy and safe. All was well. Right now she was probably falling and spinning faster than anyone had ever done, but right now she was alive. And right now she could just do the next thing she needed to do, refusing to worry about the ground and its rapid approach. Maybe she couldn't control the future, but she <u>could</u> control her present experience. Rather than giving into frightful thoughts, she could just relax and enjoy the falling, spinning motion.

"Fall and spin, fall and spin," she thought. "Faster, slower, it does not matter. Everything is all right. There is nothing to fear." As she continued her melodic, peaceful, reassuring thoughts, her spinning free-fall finally slowed.

As she became weightless, the rushing currents of air that moments ago were screaming by, began to reverse her earthward plunge, but this time the reversal was not violent. Her body was still drawn into a ball and the surface over which the wind could catch her was minimized. She began to rise and spin, lazily, much like a beach ball caught in a rising wind current. As the spinning motion subsided, she carefully extended her arms and legs, using them as stabilizers. As her motion slowed, she resumed the skydiver's position, which allowed her to see an apparently shrunken Carmine and Fidget waving excitedly in her direction. She next saw Gandor and Sarah flying up to meet her. Like a yo-yo with a one thousand foot string, Sally had returned to an elevation of just over two thousand feet.

"I wonder what happened to Sarah in that updraft," Sally thought idly. "She must not have been caught by it, or maybe she was caught by it but knew what to do with it. After all, she is a bird," her wandering exhausted mind continued its idle musing. **Suddenly, she remembered Gabby!**

"Gabby! Gabby!" she cried. "Are you all right Gabby?" Now she <u>really</u> was concerned. "After all we have been through, how <u>could</u> he be all right?" she thought fearfully, and felt herself losing altitude again. She waited for his answer. It did not come. Her heart sank, but she knew she didn't have the luxury to allow a frightening picture to form in her mind. Her fall reaccelerated, but abruptly, she forced herself to modify her thinking. "Gabby may need my help. I <u>must</u> keep my cool. He <u>will</u> be all right. My job now is just to get us down safely! I know that Gabby is safe and well." Her fall once again decelerated as these more affirmative thoughts began to take affect, and then she felt something move! "Gabby," she cried. He was still there! "Are you all right Gabby?" she repeated.

"I'm all right," he sounded weak and far away. "But please get us down quickly, and please do it carefully. I don't feel so well. I think I'm going to be sick." If it weren't for his gray hair, Gabby would have been greener than an Irish pub on St. Patrick's Day. When Sally was in her spin he <u>had</u> lost his grip, but at the last second he managed to slide into the large, back pocket of Sally's overalls. One thing for sure, he had no intention of leaving the safety of her pocket until they were back on the ground. He'd suddenly lost all interest in the view from two thousand feet.

Sally had had enough too. She carefully dialed the rheostat to fifteen pounds, trimmed her skydiver pose with her arms out and her legs up, and began to fall to the ground, accelerating to a respectable sixty miles per hour. Passing by Sarah and Gandor, she called to them "See you on the blanket in a few!" Her old confidence having returned, a broad smile came to her face, as she realized that everything really <u>was</u> going to be all right, and that everyone really <u>was</u> safe.

Chapter XI

THE LANDING

Sally adjusted the imaginary rheostat until her weight and the wind's resistance were balanced; just enough to slow but not stall or reverse her safe return to solid ground. Fidget and Carmine looked up in amazement while Sally made final corrections. Initially she adjusted her weight to read three pounds, - about that of a large beach towel. Then, as she settled down to less than ten feet from the blanket, she turned the little nob on the rheostat to read just one ounce, and fell the rest of the way like a leaf falling from a tree. Fidget, thinking he was about to be squashed, ducked, as the large Sally-leaf floated down on top of him. Not concerned that her ultralight weight could hurt anyone, but not wanting to frighten Fidget, any more than she'd already done, Sally pushed away from him with both hands. The force of the push, being way more than she needed, sent Sally flying skyward again, only to do yet another somersault before she lazily came to rest on the top branch of the nearby weeping willow tree.

"Oh phooey!" she complained. "I've had about enough of this foolishness for one day!" She turned up the rheostat to read two pounds and slid gracefully down the drooping willow branches to the ground. Having ended her air travel with a perfect stand-up landing, she quickly restored her weight to her usual sixty-five pounds, and was immediately reintroduced to the crush of earth's gravity. "I feel like a one-ton behemoth!" she thought, as she began lumbering toward the blanket. "I had no idea I was so heavy!" The added weight got Gabby's attention, too, as he was scrambling to get out of his hiding place. Feeling the squirrel wriggle in her back pocket, Sally was reminded of his presence there, and of the close call that the two of them had just experienced. Turning red with embarrassment, all she could think to say was, "Gabby! You can come out now!"

"Let me out of here!" scolded Gabby, as only a squirrel can do Without even turning to look at Sally he jumped out of her back pocket and scurried off toward the blanket.

"Gabby, I'm sooo sorry. I know you got very frightened and air sick. It was all my fault. I will never do that again. Is there anything at all that I can do to make it up to you?" Sally pleaded.

Much relieved to be on the ground, Gabby quickly stopped his scolding, and remembered the thrill of the wild ride. His mixed emotions were similar to those of a person who has gotten off their first roller coaster ride. With the ride over, terror and motion sickness often get rapidly replaced with an urgent desire to do it again. So it was with Gabby. Almost in the same breath he had used to scold Sally, he began pleading. "Yes, yes! You must take me again. Let's do it again!"

"Oh Gabby. You <u>are</u> too much!" Sally was relieved that her friend was safe, happy, and held no grudge. She also owed Fidget big time, but before she could begin to apologize, Fidget was hopping up and down in front of her in a state of unrestrained excitement.

"Ah flew, Ah flew," Fidget said, speaking faster than he ever had done before. "Sal, Ah'm ready! Ah flew on mah own, but Ah want ta be able ta do it jes like you. Ah feel more alive now than ah've ever felt! Ya promised, so Ya got ta show me how to do it. Ya jes got ta show me!"

Sally had never heard him string so many words together in one breath. Fidget was so excited he actually sounded like Gabby. Sally thought in silent amazement, "Boy did I get off the hook! Gabby and Fidget should be mad at me. Instead they want more?!"

"Si, Si. Yo tambien! I want to fly too!" Carmine exclaimed, breaking into Sally's sudden sense of relief. "I'm not as sure about this flying business as Gabby and Fidget seem to be, but it does look like fun, and I sure don't want to be left ---"

Suddenly there was the rustle of frantically batting wings and a victorious "Honk! Honk!" Gandor was coming in for a landing on the blanket, throwing his usual decorum to the wind. For the first time in his life he understood why his fellow honkers honked. They were happy! and right now he was one happy honker! "Honk! Honk! Honk!" he continued, unwilling to stop and temporarily unable to say anything else.

Right behind Gandor came Sarah, quiet and respectful. Making no sound other than that of her beating wings, she gently settled on Sally's shoulder and stood in silent attention, as proud as a mother raven who had just taught her offspring to fly.

Following Sarah's lead, the other animals turned to Sally, reverently sharing in her magnificent moment of accomplishment. Sally in turn was awestruck by the unconditional trust that she could see coming from her companions' faces. Animal limitations aside, she could tell that they were prepared to do what had earlier seemed impossible. Even Fidget stood bravely and powerfully with his furry chest out and ears erect in determined attention. The animals still did not know how they could possibly help Sally, but they were unified by their love for her and by the magic power that they had just witnessed. Confident that the way would be revealed, they looked at each other, as life-long and steadfast teammates might do, waiting for Sally's instructions.

Chapter XII

TEAMMATES

F ear began to rise in Sally's throat for the responsibility that was now placed before her, and then she remembered Gandor's warning about fear being the only real enemy. After what had just happened to her she knew that what Gandor had said was true. She felt herself letting go once more, just as she had done when she was spinning out of control. A serene feeling of peace, trust and acceptance came over her, her eyes filled with joyful tears, and a clear picture formed in her mind of her and her friends' destiny. She had been given the magic needed to fly. She could train her newly committed teammates to do it too. They would <u>fly</u> to the river together! Somehow, even though she had only begun to imagine the how, they would be given the magic needed to do the seemingly impossible things that lay ahead.

Suddenly the reverie was broken by Gabby, and then they all chimed in.

"Did you see Sally and me dive?! I felt like I was attached to a rocket!"

"Yup, Ah saw ya all right, and Ya <u>looked</u> like you'd been attached to a rocket when ya got down. But hey, did ya see mah solo flight? Ah was flyin' like a bird!"

"Salee flyees fastair than any baird. Gandor and Ahee, vee teach Salee vary wail!"

"Sally, will you teach us how to do it now too? I want to be the world's first flying coyote!"

"Yes, Sally, teach us now!"

"Hold on Gabby, give Sally a chance to breathe. She has already had a very strenuous day."

"That's OK, Gandor. I don't mind. The magic is working. I can feel it! I will teach each of you how to do it, but first there is the matter of pie! Anybody want to join me?"

That did it. Food cast its spell once more. Mrs. Martin's pie awaited. Silence descended as the party waited for Sally to cut the pie. Because Carmine and Gandor were partial to the apples, while Gabby and Sarah preferred the crust, Sally divvied the pie up accordingly. She saved a big piece for herself and Fidget to share, but apple pie really wasn't Fidget's thing. He liked apples all right, but all that cinnamon, nutmeg and sugar made his nose ache and his ears curl after a few bites. Knowing this, Sally reached into the basket and gave Fidget a delicious red apple to gnaw on for his dessert.

Unable to stop herself from feeling a little grandiose at that moment, Sally announced, "While you are finishing your lunch I will tell you how I fly!"

"Oh yes!" said Gabby, Fidget, and Carmine in unison. Gandor and Sarah said nothing but looked at each other with pride, as their student began to teach what she had learned. Gandor was especially proud to watch his protégé confidently take the role of teacher.

"First you must believe that you <u>can</u> do it! No, wait a minute, that's not right," Sally corrected herself. "You must <u>know</u> that you can do it. There can be <u>no</u> doubt in your mind at all. It took me months and months of practice before I reached that necessary state of knowing. I visualized myself flying every day. In my mind I saw, felt, heard, smelled, and tasted what it would be like to fly with nothing but air between me and the ground. The second thing you must do is eliminate all fearful thoughts from your minds. At first the thought of floating in thin air frightened me a lot, but eventually, after many months of mentally rehearsing it, I got used to the idea. To fly you must not be afraid of anything. You simply cann<u>ot</u> have even the tiniest fearful thought about anything at all, or you will not be able to do it. What's more, once you are airborne, your life <u>depends</u> on being fearless and staying that way. As you just saw for yourselves, I learned <u>that</u> one the <u>hard</u> way. Eliminating fear is a very difficult thing to do, but it is not impossible. There are many things in life that we do without fear, even though, if we let ourselves think about them as frightening, they would be. Take me for example, I walk without fear, but, if I was just now learning how to do it for the first time, it would be very frightening. Likewise, you two," Sally turned to look at Sarah and Gandor. "You fly without fear, but think how scary that would be, if you were a full-grown bird who had yet to try its wings."

Gandor began to wonder how Sally could be so wise. He was impressed that she had taken to heart so much of what he had told her, but there was more. It seemed that she had an even deeper understanding of faith and its opposite, fear, than even he had come to appreciate.

Carmine "wolfed" or more accurately "coyoted" her pie in one bite, as was her canine custom to do. She then stopped her pacing and bravely stepped forward to say, "If all you need to do is be completely unafraid and know with absolute certainty that you can do it, then I'm out of here. Mira!"

Carmine closed her eyes, and looked as though she were about to float into the air when Sally shouted "Carmine! Don't do it! You don't know how to get back down! I have not told you that part yet. Anyway, we shouldn't try it here. It is not safe. We need to practice in my Grandfather's barn where there is a roof to keep us from floating away, and where there is some soft hay to fall into if someone loses it."

"What is so hard about getting down? Can't you just think "down" and you're down? Carmine was disappointed but quickly stopped her attempt at flight.

"No you can't," Sally replied. "That doesn't work. You must adjust your weight, and that's a little more complicated than it sounds. I will explain it later, but all of a sudden, I'm exhausted! I guess all the excitement is catching up with me. Let's take the blanket under the willow tree and let our food digest before we do anything else. I can take a nap there while the rest of you visualize yourselves floating in air. Be careful though. Don't go too far with it while I'm asleep. You already saw how dangerous it can be."

"Don't worry Sally," said Gandor. "I'll watch out for everybody. You can sleep while Sarah and I help Carmine, Gabby, and Fidget prepare themselves for flying."

"Thank you Gandor." Sally picked up the picnic basket and the blanket and walked toward the shade of the willow tree. The noon day sun and the slight Santa Ana breeze had warmed the picnic spot but the cool shade of the willow tree was perfect for a nap. While the others got ready for their flying lessons, Sally stretched out on her back with her hands behind her head, and for a few minutes gazed up through the leaves of the willow at the blue sky and clouds drifting by. Then she closed her eyes, recalled herself floating in that same beautiful sky, and dreamed.

Chapter XIII

The Transformation

Dreams are usually colorless, nonsensical, blurry, confusing, and hard to remember. At first Sally's dream was like that. Out of focus, black and white images, changed right before her eyes. Things started out normal enough with Sally lying there looking up at the sky, but then the blanket began rocking back and forth, and rising into the air along with surrounding trees and houses. It was as though bits and pieces of the valley had learned to fly, but the trees were the oddest things. They glided on the breeze with their roots trailing behind. The long branches of hundreds of willows waved at Sally, with an entire orange grove leading the way, marching along like a regiment of soldiers going off to battle. As the willows and the orange grove faded from view, Mr. and Mrs. Martin passed by, nonchalantly, as though they had flown in this manner all their lives.

They too waved and called to Sally saying: "Nice day, isn't it?" But before Sally could say a word in reply, they disappeared, along with the orange grove, willow trees, and houses.

Sally thought: "This reminds me of a scene from the 'Wizard of Oz,' but it's <u>much</u> more annoying. <u>Why</u> am I moving so slowly?!" Her speech slowed down too, like one of her grandfather's old phonograph records playing at the wrong speed. The harder she tried to catch up to everyone, the slower things became. She felt like she was trapped in a vat of Jell-O while everyone else freely passed by.

Exhausted and ready to give up, Sally heard a strange commotion behind her. Faintly at first, but rapidly heading her way, she heard "Fahr'd harch! Hup, too'p, thri'p, fhar!, Hup!, too'p, thri'p, fhar. Close dem ranks ya bunnies! Ah want ya ta look sharp fer da reeview with Genera' Sal! Ah'ees-raa'it!"

Sally watched in amazement as Fidget led rank after rank of his jack-rabbit squadron past her. At Fidget's command, thousands of rabbits, all dressed in flight gear, turned their heads to face Sally and saluted. Rabbits filled the sky, each one with respectful eyes-right in tribute. As the military review continued, Sally could hear a marching band playing in the distance. In a second column to her right Gabby approached her, dressed in a drum major's uniform and leading a squirrel brass band of infinite proportions.

Just when the din was getting to be unbearable, and the parade of Gabbys and Fidgets seemed as though it would never end, there was a chorus of "Cuidado! Mira! Mira! Vamanos Sally! Run for your life! The lions are coming!" Higher in the sky and coming from the opposite direction were thousands of Carmines, shoulder to shoulder, all in one line, calling down to Sally to save herself.

Following the Carmines came thousands of snapping, roaring mountain lions in hot pursuit. Then, just when it seemed that the lions were about to overtake the coyotes, the lions stopped and turned their burning red eyes in Sally's direction, where, by looking past her, they spied the rabbits' aerial march below.

"Sallee, Sallee, Fidgeeet is falling," shreeked a gigantic flock of Sarahs in unison. The ravens flew in the opposite direction, forming a black curtain between the lions and the rabbits. *But too late!* The sight of the mountain lions had already terrified the rabbit brigade, and of course, they all began to fall.

"Well this is ridiculous! Talk about things getting out of hand! Surely I can do better! This dream is stupid, and except for the red eyes on those lions, it's not even in color!" At times Sally was very clear that she was dreaming. At other times she wasn't so sure, but just thinking the scene was stupid caused it to fade. The rabbits, squirrels, coyotes, mountain lions, ravens, and even the blanket she was floating on dissolved into an empty blackness, leaving her suspended in a dark void.

She was completely and horribly alone. As far as the eye could see there was nothing; not a speck of dust, nor movement of any kind. Except for her own breath and heartbeat, there was no sound. There was no sensation of warmth or cold. She could see her arms and hands, the end of her nose, her legs, and her feet, but nothing else. No matter where she turned, up, down, front, back, side to side, it was all the same, black and empty. As she began to think that her fear of drifting into space had come true, the terror that only a nightmare can bring left every neuron in her body in a state of red alert.

Rather than give in to the panic that was surging through her, Sally focused her attention on her annoyance once again, and was about to express her aggravation by shouting "Where is Gandor when you need him?" when she heard a friendly "Honk! Honk!" in the distance. She turned in the direction of the goose's call to find her friend flying in her direction.

"It's all right," he called to her. "There is nothing to worry about. Stay right where you are. I'll be right there. I want to show you something."

As Gandor approached, Sally droned to him in a strangely modulating voice. "Where are we, Gandor?" Her vocal chords were returning to normal, but she still sounded like Darth Vader trying to speak in falsetto. "What is this place?" she continued, her voice ramping up in pitch.

"Look down there," Gandor said, "and tell me what you see."

"Oh my! It's the earth! We <u>are</u> in space! What do we do now?" The Earth, looking to be the size of a bowling ball, was blue, smeared with white clouds, and beautiful.

"Now look above you!" Gandor exclaimed, sharing the planetary show with Sally.

The cratered moon slowly rotated <u>beneath</u>, making Sally's "up" now "down." The lunar surface was bathed in golden

Earth glow, and was outlined on one side with back-lighting from the eclipsed sun's corona. The giant Sea of Copernicus spread out in all directions like a pocked, frozen lake, and the towering peaks of its highland craters stood in stark relief on the distant horizon. At the same time, Earth turned imperceptibly far below her, but she could still make out the West Coast of North America slowly merging into twilight. Orion, Canis Major, Auriga, and Gemini, familiar constellations Sally had learned from her parents, were barely visible among the myriad stars. Sally felt she must be experiencing the same awe-struck feelings the astronauts felt on their first lunar voyage.

"Now we're getting somewhere," she said to herself, still fully aware at times that this was a dream. "We've got color, and an incredible view. I can't wait to see what happens next!"

"Okay Sally. Follow me then." Responding to her thoughts, Gandor flapped his giant wings and quickly moved across the face of the moon toward the Earth. Sally, struggling with her Jell-O like confinement, watched, as Gandor faded from view.

"Wait Gandor. Wait for me!" With all her strength and with a cry of "Let me out of here!" she finally broke free of her gelatinous prison. Streamlining her body, she pointed herself in the direction of the faded image, and willed herself through sheer dream power to the edge of Earth's oxygen atmosphere. Just in time too, since she had almost lost her winged friend, who was already making his way through the clouds.

Sally could just make him out, but his form seemed changed. He no longer looked like a bird, more like a man with a cape. And then a <u>really</u> strange thing happened. *She began to feel her<u>self</u> becoming larger.* She could see her hands getting bigger, and she could feel her face, body and legs growing too. "What's going on with me?" she cried. "And how did I end up wearing these strange clothes?"

They were through the clouds and flying over snow-capped mountains fringed with Sequoia pines, beautiful lakes, rivers, waterfalls, granite cliffs, and canyons. On and on the splendors unfolded. The scene distracted Sally from the changes that were taking place with her and her friend Gandor, who was now only a few feet ahead.

Suddenly, what seemed normal just moments before was odd. Of course she was larger. She had been this way for years. She was an adult, nearly 23 years old. Of course Gandor looked like a man. He was her very best friend.

Now convinced that she had just awakened from a dream, Sally abruptly changed her perspective. "That <u>was</u> a strange dream! How funny I would think of myself as a little girl in overalls. How odd I would think Gandor to be a goose. Boy I hope he isn't offended. Well, I don't have to tell him about it."

Gandor turned to speak to Sally. His white turtleneck sweater contrasted sharply with his long brownish gray cape, dark tanned skin and black hair. He had a commanding look with intense brown eyes that gave Sally a feeling of great confidence. His broad smile let Sally know that he was having a grand time.

"Come on Sally. We're almost there." Sally's auburn hair flowed down the back of her blue, Lycra jumpsuit. With her slender up-turned nose, high cheek bones, and radiant smile she looked like a model in a Nike sports commercial. Her green eyes joined Gandor's brown ones to assure him that she was with him and ready to see his surprise. Flying beside Sally, Gandor grabbed her left hand, and with an earsplitting drake-like grin, led her in the direction of a silver-flecked, deep-blue ribbon that was winding its way between the mountains that rose directly ahead.

As the next feature of the dreamscape came into clearer focus, Sally could see that the blue ribbon was a river calmly making its way through a pass in the pine covered mountains, and that the silvery flecks were from reflected sunlight dancing off the water's surface. Diving down to follow the course of the river at a height of about fifty feet, Sally's curiosity grew. Gandor turned to Sally, gleefully raised his eyebrows, further exaggerated his already impossibly broad grin, and nodded excitedly. "It's just around the corner!"

And then she heard it; dimly at first, but growing rapidly in decibels, as they approached the sheer granite cliff that forced the next bend in the river. At first it sounded like water gently splashing in a little stream, but as they got closer, she could tell it was much more than that. Quiet, high pitched, soprano sounds were replaced by much more ominous, low-pitched, bass sounds. As they rounded the bend, Sally's heart stopped. Before her were an unbelievable series of towering waves, crowding in one after the other in a seemingly endless cascade. Immediately she knew that this not-to-be-denied torrent was -------.

Chapter XIV

THE OUTFITTERS

"Blam!!"

Sally woke with a start. "What was that?!!" Bolting straight up in bed, Sally turned in the direction of the noise.

"Dang it! Ah fell over mah shoes and hit mah head on the confounded dresser!" exclaimed the shadowy figure.

"Fidget! Fidget!" Sally cried. "I had the most amazing dream! Can you believe it? You were a rabbit! And there was Gandor, Gabby, Carmine, and Sarah, and they were all animals too! I saw the river I've been talking about, Fidget, and I know where it is! I flew over it with Gandor! I actually know how to -."

"Hold on, hold on!" her husband interrupted. "Ah almost killed mahself here, and Ah have no idea what you're talkin' about. Give me a minute ta clear mah brain, and you can talk to me about it over breakfast. Anyway, it's time for us to get up and get ready for work."

"Yes, let's get ready," agreed Sally. "I can hardly wait to get to work and tell everyone about my dream!"

Sally Reynolds and Fred Getz, whom everyone called Fidget because he had a few persistent nervous habits, had been married for six months. Sally first met Fred in high school. They got to be good friends, and then went to college together at UC Irvine. Eventually they started dating and finally decided they were ready for marriage. Sally and Fidget both loved water sports, and now worked together at Extreme Whitewater Corporation, an outfitting Company based in Sacramento. Their Company ran guided raft tours over most of the Class V rivers in California; the designation Class V being reserved for rapids that can be "safely" navigated by only the most experienced crews. The Company also guided canoe trips on much gentler Class III rapids throughout the state, but was best known for its daredevil whitewater adventures, and was especially sought out by the most experienced and hardy enthusiasts.

"What's on tap fer ta'day?" Fidget asked. "That blow on mah head really sent me for a loop. I can't remember anythin'."

"You just haven't woken up yet. You're always like that in the morning. Why don't you take your time getting up rather than charging out of bed the minute you open your eyes? One of these days you're going to break something," Sally said, sounding like she had been married to Fidget for much longer than the actual six months. "Anyway, for your information, we're supposed to be getting ready for an easy two day paddle-boat trip down the North Fork

American and Giant Gap. Half the trip is relatively easy, but the rest of it is pretty exciting. We ran it last year, remember?"

"Oh yeah. It's all coming back to me now." As he was waking up, Fidget's native born-in-Tennessee accent left him and he reverted to the speech pattern that years in California had taught him. "Professor Johnson is scheduled to take twelve members of his ecology class from UC Davis on that run," he continued. "They've been gearing up for it all year. Ah think he said they had been on five advanced trips already. Our first day on the Chamberlin Falls run will just prime them for the thrill of their lives. Those monster waves on Giant Gap will really get their adrenaline pumping. They just have no idea. It's always fun watching novices go from terror to jubilation!"

"Come on you sadist, let's go make our breakfast. I'm dying for a peanut butter and mayonnaise sandwich," Sally said with a grin.

"A peanut what?! Why on Earth would ya want ta eat somethin' like that? And, to top it off, why would ya want it fer breakfast?" Fidget flared his nose, curled his upper lip, and looked like he was about to gag.

"I ate them when I was a little girl. I haven't had a peanut butter and mayonnaise sandwich for years, but I dreamed about it last night. I tell you that dream was a humdinger. It was so vivid! I've never had one like that before. Most of it was in color, and the characters were so lovable; especially you! You really looked good as a rabbit. I guess it's the way you flare your nose and wiggle it when you get nervous that got my dream-maker cranking on that one."

"Sally, you never cease to amaze me. I never know what you'll come up with next. Peanut butter and mayonnaise! Why I can hardly say the two words in one sentence much less eat 'em together. How in the world did you come by that one? And while we're at it, what about your making me into a rabbit?"

Fidget paused, pretending to think about his own question for a minute, and then he laughed saying. "Hmmm, on second thought, Ah guess Ah do act like one sometimes. Anyway, ya say Gandor and the other members of our team were animal characters in your dream too? If'n that's true, I guess Ah can't be <u>too</u> offended. What kind of animals were <u>they</u> anyhow?"

"Well, Gandor, he was a goose."

"Aha! I knew it! I finally coaxed it out of him the other day. Gary told me that he named himself 'The Great Gandor' when he was a little boy doing magic tricks for the neighborhood, and the nickname Gandor stuck. Unfortunately, he doesn't like it much when people change it to Gander or Gandy for short. It's hard not to do that though. When he wears his cape over a turtle neck, he looks a lot like one'a them Canadian honkers!"

"I didn't know that about his nickname," Sally replied. "I always wondered how 'Gary Masterson' got shortened to Gandor. You almost never hear his real name, and a lot of people don't even know the 'Gary,' much less the

'Masterson.' Anyway, in my dream Gary <u>was</u> a Canada goose, and a wonderful one at that. He saved my life and helped me find my river!"

"Ah want to hear more about that, that's fer dang sure," assured Fidget, exaggerating his Tennessee accent for emphasis, "but what about Gabby, Carmine, and Sarah? Who were they in your dream?"

"Well, Gabby was a chatterbox squirrel."

"That fits Mr. Gabriel Christopher to a 'T.' He can't ever stop talking, and he's got those cute little chipmunk cheeks. The coonskin cap he always wears on a river trip doesn't hurt either. So far you're doing a great job of type-casting!"

"And Carmine was a coyote," continued Sally.

"If'n it had been mah dream, she'd've been a fox, but coyote ain't bad. Carmine Castenada is almost as good looking as you are, and she's very quick and cagey. She should be very happy with the role you came up with for her. Okay then, if Carmine is a coyote, what must Sarah be? Mmmm, let me guess. I'd say Sarah was a raven."

"No kidding, you think I'm better looking than Carmine? Why thank you Fidget. In my opinion Carmine is the prettiest girl in town. That's quite a compliment!" Sally leaned over the mayonnaise jar that she was dipping into on the breakfast table and gave Fidget a kiss on the forehead. As Fidget began to pour milk into his bowl, Sally added, "How'd you know what Sarah Blackstone was like in my dream?"

"Well, gee, could it be her black hair and the black clothes she always wears? Or maybe its that fake foreign accent of hers, where she tries to imitate Steve Martin. If a raven were speaking, I'd imagine it would have an accent that would sound sort of goofy like that. Anyway, Carmine can't hold a candle to you. You have no idea how smashingly good looking you are."

"You flatter me, but then that's why I married you, and you're also quite a good detective. A raven is exactly what Sarah was in my dream, but you better not make fun of her. She saved your life! You were about to fall on your head from five hundred feet, and, if it weren't for her calling 'FEEEGEEET!' Gandor would not have gotten to you before you hit the ground. And while we're talking about it, you better be nice to Gandor too. You would have been rabbit squash, if he hadn't grabbed you by your cute little bunny tail in the nick of time."

"Ouch! I bet that <u>would</u> have hurt! Now you've really got me curious. How'd I find myself five hundred feet in the air anyhow?"

As Sally ate her breakfast sandwich and Fidget downed his bowl of cereal, she proceeded to relate her dream. Fidget sat for thirty minutes straight, bouncing his leg up and down, completely enraptured with Sally's tall tale. She was just getting to the part where Gandor was showing her the magic river, when Fidget jumped up and excitedly sputtered "We've got to get to work! We're late!!"

"Oh my golly! I completely forgot the time. We <u>do</u> have to hurry!"

Sally ran to the bedroom, threw her bathrobe on the bed, briefly ran herself under the shower, took a stab at brushing her teeth, smeared on some deodorant, climbed into her blue jumpsuit, put on her Nike Airs, tied her hair in a ponytail, and in less than ten minutes went charging out the front door of the apartment. Fidget was already in the driver's seat of their forest-green, 2005, Grand Cherokee, waiting at the curb with the engine running. He had dressed quickly in hiking boots, blue jeans, tank top, and brim-to-the-rear, "Extreme Whitewater" company cap.

Fidget called to Sally; "You forgot to close the front door! Hurry and lock up. You've got a lot to do today to get prepared for our trip tomorrow!" He nervously tapped his fingers on the car roof.

Sally shouted back as she was locking the door, "I thought you were still in the house getting ready! Anyway, what's this stuff about <u>my</u> having a lot to do? What about you? How did you get so high and mighty? I suppose you think that you get to take it easy this morning? I hope you don't expect to sit around and watch the rest of us work today!"

"No, but that would be nice. Thanks for the offer!" Fidget loved to tease Sally, and she him. They had grown close and comfortable with each other's moods and idiosyncrasies. Fidget grinned, flared and wrinkled his nose, pressed his palms together to flex his biceps and chest muscles, and musically beeped the horn along with his finger rhythm just to impress Sally.

"Fidget! Its 7:30! You'll wake the neighbors!"

"Ah know, but yer worth it," he said wiggling his nose and ears, and trying to imitate a rabbit with a toothy grimace.

Their commute would be a long one. The Sacramento morning traffic was just beginning to build. By the time the tardy couple made it to the freeway they were faced with bumper to bumper gridlock, compliments of El Nino, whose rains had slicked the pavement but also made the slow traffic more bearable by decorating the freeway center divide with plenty of April flowers.

"You know, Fidget," said Sally as they drove down the freeway. "I appreciate the time you took listening to my dream, and your willingness to understand its significance to me. I don't know the reasons for it yet, but there is no doubt in my mind that it means I must do a trip you won't approve of. I know it makes no sense, but there is no question that the river Gandor led me to in my dream is the Sanderson, and there is no way around it, I must make it all the way through the Gorge with Amber."

Dumfounded, Fidget blurted in amazement, "The Necromancer?!"

Fidget used the name given to the Sanderson Gorge by one of its recent victims. His shock was genuine.

"No one can do that gauntlet of whitewater in a canoe, especially not your wooden one!" he carried on. "Only a few people have even tried it in a raft or kayak, and they didn't do well at all! I know you've been talking about doing something crazy like this for months, but neither

you nor anyone else can make it safely through that part of
the Sanderson. Once you are in the Necromancer, you're
strictly in X-rated territory. Everyone I know characterizes
it as a one-way trip to Hell. Ya have little enough hope of
making it in a kayak, and there is just none at all for you
in Amber. Why couldn't you at least give yourself half-
a-chance by considering a kayak? Even then you could
end up with a broken neck like the fellow who tried it last
year. That stretch of the Sanderson is an eddy-less, fifteen
mile-long storm sewer. If the waterfalls don't get you, the
monster waves and bottomless holes will. Not only that,
the sheer granite walls of the Gorge leave almost no place
to recover when you lose it. And get this Sally, there is no
doubt at all, you will lose it! I know you've been obsessing
about a trip on some imaginary river for months, but I
didn't pay much attention, especially when you started
calling it a magic river. I just thought you were kidding!
Well, you're right about one thing. The Sanderson Gorge is
magic, but the magic is all from the dark side of the force!"

"Fidget, believe me. I don't know why. I know it sounds
crazy. I know I'll probably spend more time swimming
for my life than canoeing. I know Amber could be
destroyed, and I know that I'll be running a risk of
serious injury or even death. I agree that it makes no
sense, but nevertheless, I know, without any hesitation,
that I have to do it. It's like Gandor said in my dream. It
will be extremely dangerous and life threatening, but if I
don't do it, there is something that is far more dangerous
waiting for me. I don't know what it is, but I know that
it's there. Facing the fear of canoeing the Sanderson, and
conquering the river's force, is somehow connected with
overcoming this even greater threat. The trust that I felt

in my dream is <u>all</u> that I am going on to know that this is the right thing for me to do. This is the only explanation I can give for my obsession with the next-to-impossible."

Seeing that Sally hadn't been swayed by his previous lecture, Fidget once again tried to reason with her: "It's not <u>next</u> to impossible it <u>is</u> impossible Sally. Many of the waves in that gorge are more than fifteen feet high, and if you get caught in one of those treacherous holes, you'll never get out! I know from a distance it <u>looks</u> like it ought to be fun, but even the most experienced have had a bad time in those rapids. That poor fellow last year got slammed up the side of the granite cliffs with such force that his inflatable cataraft split its seams. And don't forget all the rocks and boulders; you're bound to hit a lot of them. Think about poor old Amber, it'll be like having one traffic accident after the other with her! Ya might as well take her over Niagara Falls!"

"I know, I know, but I also know I've got to do it. I must admit though, there <u>is</u> one thing that has me a little worried. In my dream, Gandor said that he and you, as well as Gabby, Carmine, and Sarah, would be helping me. It's funny. I couldn't understand at the time how a rabbit, goose, raven, squirrel or coyote could possibly be of any help. Nevertheless, I just accepted that you would somehow be able to do it, and presto, here you are, the five best whitewater guides in the business. I can't ask you to help, but that dream did leave me with the confidence that everything would be okay if you did."

"Sally, you know that I and the rest of the team will be with you no matter what crazy thing you do. Let's talk about it when we get to work. Maybe somebody will have an idea." Fidget saw that his arguments weren't getting him anywhere and had decided that humoring Sally was the best thing to do. He hoped that his teammates would talk some sense into her.

Chapter XV

DÉJÀ VU

Extreme Whitewater was located on the Northern outskirts of the city near the Sacramento River. By the time Fidget and Sally arrived there, they were two hours late. Fidget quickly parked their van and jumped out saying, "We're really going to have to hustle today!"

Gabby was on the loading dock putting gear into waterproof containers when he spotted Sally and Fidget sprinting across the parking lot. "Where have you guys been? What happened? Did you forget to wake up? Did you have car trouble? Is everything all right? I was beginning to get worried. I was going to call the police in a few minutes. No one was answering your phone. I thought you might have had a wreck or something."

Gabby's rapid-fire interrogation was interrupted by Sally. "Gabby, Gabby, calm down, calm down. Everything's all right. Its all my fault. It's just that I had the most amazing dream, and was telling Fidget about it, and forgot to watch the time."

"You're late because you had to tell Fidget about a dream? Did you forget that we were running the Gap? Why didn't ---?"

"Hold on there, Gabby," Fidget interrupted. "We know, and we're sorry that we worried you, but if you were concerned <u>then</u>, wait until you hear about Sally's dream and what she's plannin' to do. Ya won't just be <u>worried</u>. Ya'll be scared <u>stiff</u>!"

"Oh geez. Sally, please don't tell me that you've been thinking some more about that nutty, suicidal idea?"

"Ya got it Gabby," said an increasingly agitated Fidget. "Sally saw her magic river in the dream, and she's more determined than ever to run it with Amber, even if it <u>is</u> the Necromancer."

"You can't be serious!" Gabby shrieked. "There is no way that she can do that! She'll be killed or maimed for life for sure."

"It's okay Gabby," Fidget said with sarcastic assurance. "Everything will be all right. You, myself, and the others are going with her."

Gabby fell silent. He just stared at his two coworkers as though they had recently arrived from another planet. Sally, who was beginning to feel ignored, took the pause in the rapid-fire exchange between Fidget and Gabby to insert her own opinion.

"Now hold on there. Nobody is going with me that doesn't want to go. However, it <u>was</u> the Sanderson that I saw in my dream, and there's no question that the Gorge is the part of the river I've been imagining. Even though I don't understand the reason for it, I now know it's not an option for me. I must do this thing. I simply have no choice."

The color began to return to Gabby's face. He had an idea. Speaking rapidly again in his high pitched voice, he said excitedly, "I know what we need to do. Let's go get Gandor. I know you respect his opinion Sally. He'll talk some sense into you. There's no need for me to get all worked up over this. You just had a dream. You're still confused from it. There's nothing for me to worry about here. You'll see the light soon enough. Hey Gandor! Come on out here!" Gabby turned from the loading dock and headed in the direction of the office where the others were having a coffee break. "We need your help. Sally's lost her mind!"

Sally's high spirits sank. "What if Gandor doesn't support me? Fidget and Gabby think I'm crazy. Maybe I am. I've been counting on Gandor's support because he was the one who showed me the river in my dream, but that's silly. The dream was real for <u>me</u>, but I was the one having it, not he. <u>He's</u> not going to know anything about it. <u>He's</u> going to be just as shocked as the others, but if he thinks I'm crazy too, I don't think I'll be able to take it!" Her heart began pounding, and with each beat her confidence diminished until it was as though she'd never had any confidence in the first place.

Gandor emerged from the office and walked onto the loading dock. His bearing, unhesitant stride, dark hair and eyes, white turtleneck sweater, and gray cape give him a preternatural look. Sally was stunned by his appearance. He was just as she had been in her dream! Gandor's eyes found Sally's, leaving her with no doubt. Her inner voice shouted with joyful relief. "HE KNOWS!"

Gabby went running up to Gandor. "Gandy, you've got to help! Sally's really lost it! She's got it into her head to run with Amber in the Necromancer!" Gabby paused, waiting for some signs of reason and support from Gandor.

"I'm aware of that," Gandor said calmly with an amused smile.

All enthusiasm left Gabby as he saw his only hope for rational thinking join the ranks of the hopelessly deranged. "You are? How's that possible?" he whined.

"Don't worry. It just is. If I tried to explain it to you, you wouldn't believe me anyway. The Sanderson is Sally's river, she must take Amber through the Gorge, and we must help her."

"Oh no! Not you too! "Gabby was practically in tears.

"What's the matter Gabby? You don't look so good," said Carmine, who was just then walking onto the loading dock with Sarah.

"You're right. He looks like he's about to bawl. What'd you guys do to him? He was just fine a few minutes ago," Sarah agreed, glaring at her three teammates, hands on hips, in mock ferocity. With her dark eyes, short jet-black hair, black leather boots, black jeans, and black blouse, her playful intimidation was very convincing.

Gabby looked up at the two women with pleading eyes and whimpered. "Sally is going to run the Necromancer with Amber, and we're <u>all</u> going with her."

Carmine came to Gabby's rescue, "You people are terrible. You know how sensitive Gabby is. It's just not nice to tease him that way!" She moved the right arm of her olive green coveralls protectively in front of him, and let her long, dark brown hair fall back from her head to shield Gabby's face from his supposed tormentors. "Pobrecito," she consoled with soothing insincerity.

"It's no joke," said Fidget in sharp response. "She's plannin' ta canoe that death trap. Apparently she and Gandor have been cookin' this thing up. Sally first told me about the idea this morning, but Ah guess She and Gandor have had it all planned out for some time." Fidget was not happy. He was not only frightened for Sally, knowing now that she was absolutely serious, but he was also hurt to think that Sally had been planning this trip behind his back.

"Hold on Fidget," Gandor said sternly. "Sally and I haven't been cooking anything up. Believe it or not, I must have had the very same dream that she had last night. In it Sally and I flew over the Sanderson Gorge, and as we were floating over it, we both knew that there was some REAL reason why Sally had to run it with Amber. As impossible as it sounds, it's just like Sally said, everything is going to be okay. We'll do it, and we'll come out of it intact."

Gandor spoke with such sincerity and conviction that it was difficult not to believe him, although what he'd said was quite unbelievable. Gandor and Sally were highly regarded Extreme Whitewater guides. Their integrity was beyond reproach, and yet what they now were saying sounded like an impossible nightmare to the bewildered listeners. How could such a story be believed? How could anyone trust that the Necromancer could be run safely?

As Fidget, Gabby, Sarah, and Carmine stood dumbstruck, their minds rebelling against Gandor's words, a smile spread across Sally's face. Suddenly she knew what she had to do to convince her teammates that she was telling the truth. She especially wanted Fidget to know she had not deceived him. Although doubts still remained in Sally's own mind, she pushed them aside.

Sally said to herself, "This is as good a time as any. Either I believe in myself and have the strength of my convictions, or I might as well submit to their opinion that I am in fact nuts." Sally interrupted the group's befuddled thoughts with a command. "I'll show you, if you'll just help me move these inflated rafts that Sarah's been testing for leaks into the warehouse!"

Still in shock and, consequently, offering no objection, Fidget, Gabby, Sarah, and Carmine obediently began to haul four fully inflated six-man rafts from the loading dock into the warehouse. Gandor helped Sally lift one of them through the open sliding double doors of the

Quonset hut-shaped building. At the same time he leaned over and whispered in Sally's ear, "I know what you are doing."

Still smiling, Sally saw that Gandor was highly amused, and nodded to him, showing her relief at his understanding. It was Gabby, naturally, who finally broke the silence of their work.

"What do you want us to do with these rafts? Sally, I think you need mental help. You've lost touch with reality or something. Nothing you've said or done this morning has made any sense," he complained. "You keep talking about that dream. Maybe it temporarily confused your brain. Fidget, why is she acting like this? WHAT'S GOING ON HERE ANYWAY?"

"Ya got me Gabby. Ah have no idea what she's up to. Ah'm about to ask her to see a shrink. She's really gettin' me worried."

"Will you guys just relax for a few minutes," Sally said with annoyance, and then she went on to make a startling offer. "I'll tell you what," she paused for effect. "If I haven't convinced you within the next five minutes that I should go through with my plan, I'll apologize to everyone for all the trouble I've caused, and you'll have my word of honor that I will hence forth confine my canoeing to baby rapids. Deal?"

"Oh now that <u>would</u> be a deal!" exclaimed Fidget with suspicious relief. "Are you serious?" he asked suspiciously. "If ya can't convince us in the next five minutes, ya won't go through with this? Ya'll give up on this crazy notion of yours ta canoe the Necromancer, and ya'll never bring it up again?"

"You bet I'm serious. I'm willing to put it all on the line right here and now. I'll even go so far as to say that if I don't convince <u>all</u> of you, I won't do it. Five minutes from now, even if there is just one of you saying 'No Sally, don't do it,' then I won't do it. Fair enough?"

The teammates looked at each other amazed at her challenging offer, and nodded in agreement.

"You're on Sally!" Fidget exclaimed. "Go ahead and try ta convince us."

"All right then. Turn the rafts upside down and pull them together so they form a large rectangle." Sally was getting excited. Her heart pounded as she began to imagine what the next five minutes were going to be like. The little thought "What if it doesn't work" tried to insert itself, but she managed to beat it back with an "It's got to work!" and regained her authoritative confidence saying, "The four of you position yourselves so that one of you is at the each corner of the rectangle. Gandor, I want you to stand opposite me on the other side, where I can see you easily. I'm going to need all the positive energy from you that I can get."

Sally stood at the juncture between the ends of the two rafts facing her. As she stood there in silence with her eyes closed, the four confused members of the team got concerned again. "What <u>is</u> she doing?" they thought in unison, and then continued their mental anguish with various versions of "Why is she just standing there? How is this convincing us of anything?"

After several silent minutes, sweat began to appear on Sally's forehead and her expression changed from a smile to an effort-filled frown. Abruptly, she opened her eyes and startled everybody with an annoyed pronouncement. "This isn't working! I'm going to have to lie down on one of the rafts!"

Before anyone could say anything, Sally climbed up on a raft, rolled to her back, and looked straight up at the rounded ceiling thirty feet above. She also began moving her mouth and could soon be heard whispering. At first the whisper was barely audible, but as its intensity increased, the whisper rapidly transformed itself into a loud proclamation that reverberated off the aluminum warehouse walls. "I CAN DO IT! I HAVE NO FEAR! I CAN DO IT! I HAVE NO FEAR!" She repeated the dream-familiar chant over and over until she was practically screaming it.

"Oh geez!" Gabby cried, feeling sick to his stomach and becoming very frightened for Sally. "Fidget, you'd better stop her. She's really lost it!"

"Quiet!!" Gandor's eyes <u>burned</u> at Gabby. "Just stay put, watch, and keep your mouth sh - -."

Gandor didn't get to finish his command. Sarah saw it first and shouted, or rather screeched "WEEL YEW LEWK AIT THAIT!"

87

This was followed by gasping sounds accompanied by an excited polyphonic chorus exclaiming "What the - - ?", "Oh mah gawd!", "No es possible!", "I don't believe it!", and a "YES!!! I KNEW SHE COULD DO IT!!!"

Sally was floating fifteen feet above the inflated rafts. It was just like she had done in her dream, only this time no one was holding on. Her arms and legs were outstretched, and she was rigidly ascending to the top of the rounded roof. There was almost no time for her to think, however, before she had flown straight up to bang her head on the ceiling of the warehouse. Inspired by the bang on the head, a minor dose of fear skipped its way into Sally's psyche and broke her concentration.

"AAAAHHHHEEEE!" she screamed, falling toward the raft and bouncing, as though it had been planned, right into Fidget's arms.

Chapter XVI

DISTRACTING THOUGHTS

S ally looked up expectantly into Fidget's eyes saying, "Well, are you convinced?"

He was convinced all right, and so were they all. Even Gandor was impressed. At least <u>he</u> had been ready for it, but he still found it necessary to pinch himself to make sure he wasn't dreaming. Everyone stopped talking and tried to adjust to what they had just witnessed. What they saw could not have happened. Everyone knew that it was impossible, and yet, there was no escaping the fact that they had all seen Sally float twenty feet, straight up, to the top of the warehouse.

Fidget shook his head and finally found a way to speak. "I saw it, but I don't believe it. If I didn't know better, I'd think you were in cahoots with David Copperfield, Sally. It would be much easier for me to believe that you pulled off one of his levitation illusions than to accept the fact that I actually saw you fly, but I know it was no trick. You <u>did</u> actually do it! And I was right here to see it with my own two eyes!"

Fidget continued his attempt to rationalize the irrational, and in so doing he began to wonder if some other things that he had seen could <u>actually</u> be much more than advertised.

"Hey! Maybe the Amazing Randi and Masked Magician campaigns to expose the tricks of mentalists and illusionists is an occult conspiracy designed to throw people off. Maybe Copperfield's tricks aren't tricks at all?! Maybe he actually has Sally's ability to fly! And maybe Uri Geller <u>actually</u> bends spoons with his mind!"

"You're right Fidget!" Carmine chimed in. "Now that I've seen the unbelievable come from someone I know and trust, I find myself throwing all my old ideas about magic and the impossible out the window!"

Sarah interrupted. "Sally, you've got to show us how you did that!"

"No kidding!" Gabby agreed. He'd had flying dreams himself, and was always annoyed when he woke up to find he'd only been dreaming. Also, he now had a real reason to hope that Sally would lose interest in her obsession about the Necromancer. "Let's quit this rafting business and go on the road with our own flying show! The six of us would be a sensation! We could be more famous than the Beetles, Elvis, and the Pope combined! What do you say Sally? This new-found ability of yours has got to be more important to you than a crazy canoe trip!"

"Hold on Gabby!" Fidget said sternly. "Sally made a deal with us, and we all accepted it. She convinced us, just as she said she would, and now we have to honor our side of the agreement. Personally, Sally, the thought of you in a canoe on the Necromancer still gives me the heebee jeebees, but we have an agreement, and each one of us <u>will</u> hold to it. We're behind you one hundred percent. You just tell us what you want us to do. Right gang?"

"Right!" They all replied in unison.

Nearly beside himself with enthusiasm, Gandor was quick to add, "Sally, we <u>are</u> all with you! Like Fidget said, just tell us what you want us to do next."

Sally responded, feeling so buoyant she began to wonder if she might once again take flight. "Okay, but I have to tell you, - I wasn't as sure of myself as I made out to be. I'm just as amazed by what happened as the rest of you. Even though I'm <u>way</u> too befuddled to do any serious leading, I've always found that it works well just to do the next indicated thing. What do you say we continue getting ready for our trip with Professor Johnson and his Ecology class tomorrow? We've got a lot of work to do here, so let's pretend for now that nothing happened, and let's just focus on the tasks at hand. Then we can start planning our strategy to take on the Sanderson."

"Good idea," agreed a somewhat more subdued Gabby. "I guess my poor brain <u>could</u> use a break. Actually, some plain old normalcy sounds pretty wonderful right now, - but you will show us soon how to do it, - - won't you?" he pleaded, trying to get over his dashed hopes of avoiding the Necromancer.

"You bet I will Gabby, - and I think you may have something there. It would be fun to take a show on the road. Can you imagine what it would be like when people discovered for themselves that what we were doing wasn't a trick?" Sally left her teammates, especially Gabby, pondering the unimaginable, a world where everyone could fly on their own.

Without further discussion the outfitters set about their respective chores. Gabby continued his check list of hardware items to be stored in water proof containers, Fidget began packing fragile items into ammunition boxes for safe keeping, Sarah proceeded with her leak checks and raft repairs, Sally and Carmine went shopping for the necessary food items, and Gandor attended to the vehicles and entertainment plans.

Sarah, still highly charged by what she had seen, began an excited monologue about eco-politics while she worked on the rafts.

"Professor Johnson is a neat guy. I wish I'd had a teacher like him. He's really got his class motivated, and extremely incensed by the State's plans to dam more of California's wild rivers. They're particularly upset with the legislature's talk of putting a dam on the North Fork American below Chamberlain Falls. I'm sure it's no coincidence that Johnson has chosen this run for his class's final rafting trip. I'm really looking forward to making this trip a great experience for them. They've gotten to be pretty influential activists, and I don't think that any of them are going to let the issue slide by without giving it their all. I'd be willing to bet that by the time they finish the Giant Gap their adrenaline will be so pumped that they'd be willing to capture the entire State legislature, tie them to a raft, and show them first hand why damming the river is such a monstrous idea."

Chapter XVII

PREMONITIONS

The outfitters' preparations had to be meticulous. There would be no room for sloppy work. The planned run was a dangerous one. Everyone had to be prepared. Provisions and gear had to be double-checked to be sure that they were complete and in top shape.

The immediate goal was to pack, load the van and raft trailer, drive to a site near the Chamberlain Falls point of entry, pitch camp, and get ready to meet Professor Johnson and his class the following day. Since the Falls portion of the trip was actually below Giant Gap, and since they wanted to take Professor Johnson and his class on the less challenging run first, they planned to start at the midway point, then take on the Gap, and finish where they started.

This would be the Ecology group's first exposure to the beauty and challenge of the North Fork American River, and Sally and the others of the outfitting team were eager to make it a perfect trip. However, it was not an easy matter for any of the well-intentioned outfitters. All of them were having difficulty concentrating on their work.

No one talked about it, but none of Sally's teammates could get it out of their minds. They had witnessed a miracle, the dawn of a new age. They just couldn't help thinking about it, and once again their collective thoughts were practically in unison. "If Sally can do it, then I should be able to do it. It must be that we've been able to do it all along, but we've grounded ourselves with self-imposed limitations. It's just like Sally said about Roger Bannister. Until he ran the four-minute mile, many thought it couldn't be done. However, once he did it, all the top milers could do it, and many went on to exceed his record time. I wonder what else I could do, if I just didn't think I <u>couldn't</u> do it?"

Lost in these thoughts, the excitement of the team's newfound, uninhibited thinking made their work and their trip to the campsite go by quickly, but that evening with everyone gathered around the fire, Sally wondered if she had forgotten something. It was unlike her not to be able to remember every detail of her preparations, but this time, even though she had doubly checked everything, she wasn't sure of any of it. "Oh well, at least everyone else will be on their toes," she thought. Little did she know that everyone else was in the very same boat.

That night, looking into the campfire and dismissing her distracted state of mind, Sally was reminded of her dream and the lunch she had with her animal friends.

"I never got to show them how to fly," Sally lamented to herself. "Carmine so wanted to be the world's first flying coyote."

However, any longing Sally had been feeling for Carmine's previous incarnation was rapidly replaced by the frightening image of a coyote floating in air. The scary thought of her friend flying off into space, with no idea of how to get back down, was all that Sally needed to send her mind off in a different direction, but Fidget wouldn't let her leave it alone.

"Hey Sally," Fidget said with genuine excitement. "Now would be a great time to tell the others about your dream!

At first Sally was reluctant. She had just rid herself of the frightful thought, and now she was being forced to remember it again. Moreover, the dream was important to her and she wasn't sure she was ready to risk having anyone make fun of it. But Fidget and the others were looking at her with such supportive respect and enthusiasm, her reluctance quickly evaporated.

As she started telling her story and how it began with herself, as a little girl, floating in air over a beautiful valley, Sally had a second momentary panicky feeling. But this time the feeling was different. It seemed more real, more urgent, more intense, and it was accompanied by an alarming vision of a destructive force, onrushing, black. "What was that?" she wondered. The feeling and scene were out of place. They did not belong in the present setting and they were obviously unconnected to her story. Sally successfully pushed the fleeting vision and its accompanying disturbing feeling aside, and continued on with her story.

Once she started it, she could not stop. Nor did her enraptured audience make any attempt to interrupt her. They were so engrossed, that they hardly allowed themselves time to blink. The description of the dream was reinforcing their excitement over Sally's magical powers, and heightening their own desire to someday do what they had seen.

It was <u>way</u> past everyone's bedtime by the time the story finished.

"Oh gee, Professor Johnson and his class are going to be here first thing tomorrow morning. We'd better get to bed. I'm really sorry. I completely lost track of time!"

"That's okay Sally. Your story was wonderful, but why did you make me into a squirrel?" Gabby asked jokingly with his cheeks all puffed out like they were packed with nuts.

The next day, Johnson and his students arrived on time, ready to take on the rapids of the Chamberlain Falls run.

Chapter XVIII

THE DEBACLE

I t should have been a routine trip, and it should have been uneventful. But things started going wrong almost from the start.

The Professor, and his excited nineteen–member class, were in five, six-man rafts. Sally, Fidget, Gabby, Carmine, and Sarah were at the tiller of each raft. Professor Johnson rode with Sally in the lead, while Gandor brought up the rear in a kayak.

A half-mile from the put-in, the rafting party successfully navigated Slaughter's Sluice, a boulder-strewn slalom with a large midstream rock right in the middle of the rapid's entryway. Sally guided her raft to the right of the rapid, and then had the Professor and her student-crew work their way left, behind the midstream rock, for a textbook execution. The other rafts, with Gandor in his kayak, followed suit.

It was a lovely day and the enthusiastic paddlers had performed their first rapid admirably. Professor Johnson gave Sally a high-five and signaled approval to the rest of his class with a double thumbs-up. Although the roar of the downstream rapids mostly muted their excited whooping and hollering, Johnson could tell that his class was as excited as he was.

"<u>Sen</u>sational!" the Professor shouted to Sally.

Sally nodded in agreement, but her mind was elsewhere. Perhaps it was the ease with which she maneuvered through the first rapid that lulled her into thinking about flying, instead of paying close attention to the next challenge on the river. Suffice it to say, she had chosen a very inopportune time to become distracted. The next rapid was Chamberlain Falls itself, a class IV+ narrow slot with an eight-foot, vertical drop that was waiting for its unwary victims with a trap, a big, unforgiving, reversal.

Sally allowed her crew to drift their raft too far to the left, and they found themselves caught in a violent eddy between the reversal and the left bank. They simply could not get out of it. Professor Johnson was beginning to panic, and the rest of the crew no longer looked like they were having fun. The situation was already bad enough, but it was only the beginning of Sally's troubles. Most of her rafting guide-mates weren't prepared either. Gabby, Fidget, Sarah and Carmine all had visions of grandeur dancing in their heads. Their usual focus and clear-headed thinking had left them, - completely. To a man and woman they were each, along with their increasingly anxious customers, drawn like moths to a flame in the direction of Sally's demise. Later they would discuss and analyze the incident in a futile attempt to understand how a team of top whitewater guides could have gotten themselves into such a mess. Maybe it was a natural consequence of the team's unified, initial reaction to help Sally, or maybe it was an omen of worse things to come that had drawn them like a magnet into the trouble. No matter, what happened, happened, and as each crew-chief realized what was happening, their actions only drew their rafts closer to the ensnaring eddy.

There was not enough room to accommodate all five rafts. One by one the rafts swept over the falls and piled into the reversal, one on top of the other. The situation was dangerous and embarrassing, and to make the embarrassment worse, two other commercial rafting parties, parked just downstream, had front-row seats.

Chapter XIX

SCOUTS

"I still can't believe they fired us!"

"Well, what'd you expect Gabby. We blew it bigger than anyone has done in the history of rafting! Maybe it wouldn't have been such a big deal if we didn't have to be rescued!" Gandor's exaggerated response referred to the members of Wild River Challenges and Whitewater Explorations, the downstream witnesses to Extreme Whitewater's misfortune.

"You're right," Fidget agreed. "Professor Johnson and his class were first rate. If it had been up to them, we'd still have our jobs. They forgave us immediately and were great helping us get up and running again. They didn't even freak-out when they had to miss lunch because 'you-know-who' forgot to pack our food in waterproof pouches." Fidget referred, good naturedly, to Sally who finally discovered after-the-fact what she'd forgotten.

Fidget continued: "I don't know what was so funny about soggy sandwiches, but my stomach's still sore from laughing, and for a while there I thought the Professor and his class were going to require paramedics, they laughed so hard. I'm just glad no one got hurt and that we recovered enough of our equipment to complete the first half of the run. Our heads really must have been in the clouds. We didn't even have throw-lines! I know I carefully packed them, but then I must have just as carefully unpacked them. The good news is, we got help, or we <u>would</u> have been in trouble! The bad news is, all that attention got us fired. Especially after the negative press in the local papers, to say nothing about the national TV-coverage. I'll bet that Wild River guide who had the video camera made a fortune. Extreme Whitewater got so much unwanted notoriety it's no wonder they let us go."

Sarah was philosophical. "It's just as well. I was beginning to wonder how we were going to honor our commitment to Sally and at the same time represent Extreme Whitewater. There's no way the Company would have approved our trip through the Gorge, - not <u>even</u> with our own equipment. They simply would not have wanted to be associated with something so dangerous."

"As for me," Carmine added, ignoring the career-oriented postmortem, "I'm just thankful one of us was able to avoid the pileup. I was in a bad tangle, trapped under my raft. If Gandor hadn't come to my rescue in his kayak, I probably would have drowned. "<u>Muchas</u> gracias mi amigo!"

"De nada" Gandor melted. He'd been secretly admiring Carmine for months, and had put her on such a high pedestal he'd given up all hope of ever finding enough courage to let her know. Thanks to the close call the inhibiting ice had been broken.

Sally was oblivious to her teammates rehashing of the accident, and, surprisingly, didn't even show any interest in Gandor and Carmine's blooming love interest. She had her mind focused on other matters – the rapids of the Sanderson. "The past is history, tomorrow's a mystery, and today's a gift. That's why they call it the present." Sally recited the timeworn affirmation in a singsong non-sequitur, putting everyone on notice that she was intent on the task at hand. She had already taken full responsibility for the accident, and had already apologized profusely, but she remained undeterred. If anything, she was more determined than ever. "What's done is done," she continued softly. "We just need to stay focused," and then with a stern voice filled with confidence: "We said we're going to do this and by gosh we <u>are</u> going to do it. Let's finish things up here and go have a look at the Gorge."

"Yeah, let's get this over with," said Gabby, resigned to his fate. "I was about to quit rafting and start a flying career anyway!"

After the mishap, the team had quickly cut their losses. They completed the first half of the Johnson party's misadventure without further incident, returned Extreme Whitewater's equipment, suffered through the humiliating press releases, picked up their last paychecks, and followed Sally's undaunted lead, pressing on with their plans.

Now on the banks of the Sanderson, the day before the big event, they had been doing their best to scout the river's course. Although they were able to do a decent job reading the rapids leading up to the Gorge, the Gorge itself was a <u>big</u> problem. Its waters were way too chaotic to predict.

"Sally, take a look this!" Fidget exclaimed, obviously shaken. Having moved their van to a spot near the top of the Gorge, the team made a futile attempt to study the river from their new perspective. Fidget passed the only set of binoculars to Sally so that she could get a magnified view of the tortured river as it crashed its way through a bottleneck more than a half mile below. What looked like froth to the unaided eye was a gigantic boil, but it was the maelstrom behind it that caught Fidget's attention.

"Oh my. I see what you mean. It does look hopeless doesn't it? Well, that settles it, this isn't doing us any good. We're wasting our time here. All we're doing now is unnerving ourselves. There's clearly no way we can plan any of it, so let's get out of here. Anyway, we need to rest up so that we can get an early start tomorrow." Sally looked at her teammates, and gave them a forced smile. "Thanks for sticking with me. I <u>know</u> it's going to be okay," and then, she said so softly nobody could hear it: "I don't know how or why, but I <u>am</u> sure of it."

Left with nothing but faith to go on, the scouting party headed back to their van for the ride home.

Chapter XX

THE SANDERSON

The river had an easy access three miles upstream from the gorge. Here the Sanderson was deceptively peaceful as it coursed through a broad, deep channel, concealing a flow of more than four thousand cubic feet per second. The first half mile consisted of a lazy downstream float. The next two miles featured a series of class II rapids that gradually developed into something more challenging, including several class III waves, and a drop named the "Crusher." The latter, a class IV booby trap, had gotten its name from a dangerous reversal that tended to toss its victims from their crafts. The last half-mile of the run was a gentle paddle with an easy take-out just ahead of the gorge. Sally had chosen these first three miles as a self-imposed test, promising herself that she would call the whole trip off if she could not make it through this relatively "benign" section of the river without major difficulty.

Fidget lifted Amber from the top of the van, and then helped Sally carry the sleek craft to the water's edge. As he helped her get ready, Fidget wanted to say one last time that it was not too late to turn back, but he kept his mouth shut, knowing full well that any attempt to dissuade Sally was futile. Resigned, Fidget placed his hands on Sally's shoulders, gave a long, last look into her determined green eyes, and planted a loving kiss on her forehead before he turned to help his team finish their preparations.

Gandor would follow immediately behind Sally in a cataraft armed on both sides with three, coiled ranks of explosive, remotely discharged, throw-lines mounted on each of the cataraft's pontoons. A lightning-quick response would be necessary to get a rescue line to Sally before the cataraft rushed by in the roaring rapids. Failing that rescue attempt, it would be up to Fidget's team to save the day.

Gandor, was the only one other than Sally who had been looking forward to the trip. He "knew" they would be successful. He could "see" the outcome. He was not afraid for Sally, himself or for the others, and he was ready to have the time of his life. Standing knee deep in the Sanderson, and securing a blue life vest over his wetsuit, Gandor lifted his red plastic crash helmet from the seat of the waiting cataraft, gave Sally a wink and, as she stepped into Amber, urged everyone on with a "Let's go get 'em!"

In sharp contrast to Gandor's high spirits, Gabby, Sarah, and Carmine had picked up on Fidget's anxiety, and like him, were in fear for Sally's life. They, with Fidget in charge, would follow Gandor in a six-man paddle-and-oar raft, bringing with them all manner of emergency equipment and first aid. Their entire focus was on being there to support Sally's rescue, for, in their minds there could be no doubt, she would need to be rescued.

"How does Sally seem to you Fidget?" Gabby inquired with a worried look.

"She's confident," Fidget replied. "We might as well get used to it. She is going to do this thing. Let's just make sure that we are there for her when she needs us!"

"You bet," Carmen assured. "You can count on us Fidget. Vamanos muchachos!", she added with her mock Spanish accent, trying her best to keep things light and build her own confidence.

"Wey arr saam wyle dan craa zee Guys!" a Sarah-turned-Steve-Martin half-heartedly exclaimed, less able to go along with Carmine's forced air of levity.

Finished with their work, Fidget's crew brought their raft to the water's edge and stood beside Gandor, watching with mixed emotions as Sally finished her preparations.

Dressed in a white hard hat, red life vest, yellow nylon coat, black full-body wet suit, and blue diver's booties, Sally was not exactly a fashion plate for the paddling world. But such considerations were a minor issue in preparation for a serious river challenge, and they certainly were not a consideration today. With success her only consideration, Sally took one last inventory, made sure that her head gear and splash curtain were fastened securely, and from the competitive canoeist's kneeling position pushed Amber into the icy water of the Sanderson.

Un-dammed and fed by countless smaller rivers and streams that were filled with Sierra Madre, Spring run-off, the massive liquid column of blue potential-energy moved by silently like a covert juggernaut. Feeling Amber respond to the mighty stream's power, Sally understood, as if understanding it for the first time, the extraordinary challenge she was about to face. Although Amber was a C-1, decked, and designed for whitewater with every free square-inch charged with air-filled flotation, the craft, nevertheless, was still a canoe, and a wooden one at that! There would be no room for missteps.

The sky was majestically lined with thunderheads. "It looks like we're going to miss that rain after all," Sally thought. "We should be through this run and heading home in less than two hours, well ahead of any storm." Sally turned, gave a final thumbs up to Fidget and her teammates, and said aloud, "All right then," as much to let the river know of her determination as to assure herself. Then, snugging the splash-curtain drawstring a final time around her waist, she straightened to a full kneeling position, lifted the single-bladed paddle from Amber's mahogany deck, and gave the canoe a committed stroke toward the middle of the flow.

"Hey Sally! Wait for me!" called Gandor from his cataraft. Perched atop the raft chair with his double-bladed paddle he looked a little like a king with a scepter upon a water-borne throne.

Gandor's self-assurance was just what Sally needed. She remembered her dream and Gandor's lecture about fear.

She noticed that the fear was still there, but took heart in the fact that it seemed to be receding.

The six-man raft followed the cataraft into the channel. Carmine and Gabby paddled strongly, each at the front of the raft on opposite sides. Fidget manned the oars in the center, and Sarah took the helm paddle. Nobody was talking or smiling. They were simply getting the job done and wishing it to be safely over. Fidget thought Sally looked more fragile and alone than ever. He wanted to be with her, to hold her, to keep her safe, but he couldn't. He knew that he needed to be right where he was, manning the oars of the raft, ready to recover Sally when Amber capsized.

Sally was worried about the concern that Fidget and the others were experiencing, but she was also aware that this was her only remaining source of fear, and knew that she had no choice but to let it go. She could not afford a fearful thought here anymore than she could when she was flying. "If I can just stay fearless, I know I'll make it," she kept telling herself.

Amber drifted peacefully down the Sanderson with Sally paddling rhythmically from side to side, taking it easy and maintaining her course. The beauty and serenity of this section of the river were disarming. Sally smiled and took a deep breath of the clean mountain air. She was instantly rewarded with a strong scent of pine mixed with damp, river musk. A distant "screee" from a lonely red-tail hawk greeted the morning sun's break over the tree-line. This was the glorious alpine wilderness that Sally had seen in her dream, and it was all she could do to keep from slipping into a state of hypnotic euphoria. "Wake up," she alerted herself, and refocused her attention on the dangerous task at hand. Sally had become very adept at "reading" water, just as Eskimos "read" snow, and because this skill was about to become very important to her, she began to focus on it in earnest.

At first the rapids were gentle, little more than riffles, and for another mile the river continued to require nothing from Sally but rhythmic paddling. This was still the kind of fun that even a novice at canoeing could experience, but after a time the gradient began to increase, and with a quickened pace, the rapids began to grow, giving the canoe a decided bounce and splash.

"Here we go," shouted Gandor, trailing 50 yards from Sally's port side. "Hang on. We're about to get wet!"

Sally barely heard Gandor. Her mind was occupied with what she believed to be far more important matters, *but had she known that these were the last words she would hear from any of her teammates, she would have been far more attentive!*

The wave looked immense. "That's the largest class III I've ever seen," she mused. "We must be in Texas." The quickening currents of the narrowing channel pulled at Amber driving the canoe toward the depths of the threatening standing wave. The air was filled with crashing, sucking sounds emanating from tons of a nearly pure molecular substance focusing its tireless energy on whatever was in the way of its victim's ever-shrinking path of escape. "Oh my Gawd!" Sally cried. "Already I'm in trouble and I haven't even started!" She imagined her canoe diving nose first into the wave and pearling like a surfboard straight to the bottom of the river. "SALLY!" she heard her inner voice command. "THERE IS NOTHING TO FEAR!"

All of Sally's attention turned to the next few square meters directly ahead. Every drop of water became a significant detail. Much as a big league batter can see the stitching on a baseball as it whizzes by at more than a hundred miles per hour, Sally could see the water's fluid structure in freeze frame after freeze-frame. With time slowed to a standstill she saw an eddy temporarily form to the right of the wave where she could gain control for a few precious milliseconds. Now in the eddy, and back-paddling for what seemed to be many jerky, long minutes of slow motion, she timed her exit to coincide with an ebb in the towering surge. Her canoe swept through the tumult of the giant wave, and down its backside into the relative safety of froth that churned just beyond the rapid's boiling reverse wash.

Having successfully met her first challenge on the Sanderson, Sally sighed with relief and turned to view the watery churn she had just traversed. At the top of the wave came Gandor, his eyes wide and mouth open in a "Ya-Hoo!" that was made totally inaudible by the aqueous cacophony.

Sally would have liked to continue as spectator, but there was no time to watch, no time to see Gandor's landing at the end of his ride, and no time to find out how Fidget and Carmine were doing, or how the rafters came through the wave. The "Crusher" was next, and a low roar announced the fact with intense inevitability.

Chapter XXI

THE CRUSHER

Fidget's heart skipped a beat. Sally had been swallowed by the wave, having penetrated it at its very center. But then came Gandor, obviously having a splendid time, as he flew over the top, right behind Sally. "She's okay," Fidget thought. Much relieved, he turned his attention to the fact that he and his crew were about to have to ride the wave themselves. "My gad that thing's big!"

Fidget shouted forward to Carmine and Gabby, as their raft approached the swelling mountain of liquid, "This is no class III! It's <u>way</u> too big!! The river must be well over three thousand cubic feet per second. Something must be increasing the flow!"

"'Tiene' razón!", Carmine retorted. "Hay demasiado agua!"

"KERSPLAT!!" An unexpected broadside from the churn leading up to the rapid sent everyone flying to the bottom of the raft, including Fidget, who slid backwards while still hanging on to his oars.

"On Geez! We're losing it!" Gabby screamed, as they began to get sucked into the upwardly thrusting torrent.

"Paddle right!" ordered Sarah from the stern, and scrambling back to her position at the helm. "We'll have to run it backwards!"

"Hang on!!" All control was left to Fidget who had managed to regain his seat and force his oars to bring the raft around so that his back was to the menacing wall of water. "Well, we're sure off to a flying start!" And the wave began to fill their raft to the brim. "How embarrassing! How'd we let this happen anyway?"

Sarah, who was now in front, had again dropped to the bottom of the raft and was in the process of being temporarily submerged. Carmine and Gabby had hunkered down and were preparing, themselves, to be submerged. Fidget continued to man the oars and maintained the raft turned submarine on course, as it was driven through the wave and down its slope to the other side.

Water poured from the self-bailing craft as they exited the rapid like drowned rats.

"Helllooo people! We're supposed to be the rescuers!" yelled Fidget. "Let's get with it! We have just enough time to turn this thing around before we have to face the "Crusher!"

Upon regaining their forward position, Fidget scanned the river, looking for Sally. She was nowhere to be seen!

But, just then the mist boiling up from the Crusher to obscure their view, lifted, and a very excited Gabby shouted "I see her! There she is!"

"Yo tambien! I see her too" cried Carmine. "She made it!!"

"But where is Gandor?!" Sarah screamed. "He's gone!!"

Suddenly Gandor's whereabouts became a very low priority to the rafting team. The Crusher was pulling at them, and they were each going to have to focus all of their attention on surviving the new threat.

"Paddle right!" shrieked commander Sarah from her position at the stern. She was heading the raft in the direction of an eddy where they could gain some control and establish an approach to the drop.

In Fidget's mind this rapid should have been listed as a class VI waterfall and, as much water as there was flowing today, he <u>knew</u> he was right. But the rating didn't matter now. They were irreversibly committed to following through with their strategy for maneuvering the rapid. Once they were in the eddy they would spin the raft around so that it ran parallel to the face of the fall. It would then be their job to paddle and oar with all of their might to move the raft as far right as possible in an attempt to avoid an eighteen-foot vertical drop into the Crusher's maul, a reversal from which there would be no graceful means of exit.

"Paddle left!" came Sarah's command. "Now row yee swabs like yee ne'er rowed 'afore!!"

The raft slowly moved broadside to the beckoning cataract. Then, picking up speed, the raft began to plummet nose first down the Crusher's slide.

"Paddle left!" came the last futile order from Sarah. It was of no use. The raft was being drawn like a magnet toward the final drop-off.

Everyone saw it at once. Gandor's cataraft was at the bottom of the fall, churning over and over in a cascade that was hell-bent on sending everything in its path to the bottom.

"Oh no!" Gabby screeched. "We're going in too!!"

"Hang on everybody. Here we --!!!!" As Fidget's last words were cut short by the raft's sudden dive into the Crusher's gullet, the raft up-ended vertically and sent its unsecured contents and hapless occupants flying into a devouring vortex.

The Crusher's backwash was deep and, with one exception, completely unforgiving. Bodies and rafts alike were scrambled like eggs on their way to the bottom of an aqueous omelet. Fortunately, for those in the know there was a way out. Carmine was the first to recover enough to head for it. Underwater with the rest of her teammates following her lead, Carmine quickly unbuckled her life vest, a device that was already beginning to force her to the turbulent surface, and swam straight toward and under the thundering, boil at the base of the fall. At the fall's granite face she surfaced and was immediately greeted by a cheery voice. "Hi Carmine. What took you so long?"

Gandor had been sitting on the ledge under the fall with a big grin on his face watching the whole show. Through gaps in the cascading water he could see his teammates' raft and his cataraft being endlessly tortured by the pounding deluge, and he could see his friends struggling to the surface to meet him. It hadn't taken him long to adjust to the fact that his great good time on the Sanderson was over. He was already enjoying himself waiting to see what would happen next. It was always a special treat for him when things did not quite turn out as expected.

Carmine was soon joined by Gabby, Sarah and Fidget. They were glad to be alive, but little else. Some rescuers they had been!

Fidget spoke first. "Hey Gandor. Can you see Sally? What's she doing?"

"Yeah, I can see her through this break in the fall. She made it just fine, unlike the rest of us, and she's just paddling in place out there in a calm part of the river, looking up this way. I waved at her earlier, and she waved back, so I know she can see us. She's not coming this way though. I really don't know what she's up to. Wait a minute! She's turning around! She's heading for the gorge!!"

"OH NO!! SALLY! COME BACK! DON'T DO IT!" Fidget was beside himself and shouting at the top of his voice, but of course Sally could not hear him.

Chapter XXII

THE NECROMANCER

Sally could only watch helplessly with a clear knowledge of how the next events would unfold. She had navigated the Crusher successfully, and while it had not been difficult for her, she was certain that the two rafts would have problems.

From the eddy on the left side of the river, she had paddled safely in a course parallel to the mouth of the Crusher's cascading drop. Once she reached the opposing, right-hand side, she simply forced the bow of her canoe over the lip of the fall, and then with no further effort, easily rode the 20-foot drop by guiding her canoe down a seamless 100-foot chute. The force of the ride sent Amber speeding out into the Sanderson like a power boat, but her forward movement soon slowed, leaving her paddling in a river that had resumed its calm meandering way.

Sally had quickly turned her canoe around to face the waterfall, and waited for her companions' certain demise. She knew there was no way they could reach the chute on the other side of the fall, and there was no way to approach the chute directly due to the placement of boulders that lay upstream in its path. There was only a narrow passage just in front of the fall where one could reach the chute to safely navigate the drop. Any other course would end in an abrupt twenty foot dive into the reversal-of-no-return. The amount of water that was now moving over the fall would make it impossible for the clumsy rafts to reach the chute. It was hopeless and she was helpless. All she could do was watch.

Gandor almost made it. He continued paddling all the way down the initial incline and had just arrived at the edge of the chute when his cataraft flipped into the Crusher's grinding reversal.

"Shazbot!" Gandor objected to himself, as he surrendered to the unyielding force that seemed determined to drag him to a watery oblivion. Realizing there was nothing more for him to do but relax and enjoy the ride, he discarded his life jacket and just let the Crusher's undertow have its way until he felt the release of its powerful grip. Having been carried to the very bottom of the river, he pushed away from the rocky floor with his feet, flutter kicked his way to the rock face of the fall, and pulled himself up to sit on the protected ledge. Once there he was able to see Sally through a part in the curtain of water that was now crashing by in front of him, and he waved to her to let her know that he was okay.

Sally waved back and waited for the next unseating.

It was worse for the support team. The raft went nose down, mimicking the Titanic in its final exit scene. But even though contents and passengers were thrown like trash from a dumpster into a giant blender, Sally knew that all hands were safe when she saw Sarah and the others join Gandor on the ledge that nature had tucked away so conveniently under the falls.

Sally just sat there for a time, allowing Amber to drift slowly backwards down the Sanderson. She was intently studying her teammates and thinking rapidly in a stream of consciousness.

"If I go to help them, I'll never have another chance to run the Necromancer. It's now or never. I can see that Fidget and the others are okay and I know that they are perfectly capable of taking care of themselves. We left one van at the gorge take-out just in case something like this happened. They won't need my help to climb to the bank from the ledge they're on, and there's less than a half mile for them to carry whatever they can salvage. They are finished for the day, and yet I am as ready as I ever will be. I feel terrible about leaving them here, but I have no choice. I just know that this will be the only chance I'll ever get. I must go on even though there is way too much water in this river today. There must have been a really bad storm in the mountains to have increased the flow this much. Everything is going to be a lot more difficult and dangerous. What we just went through was virtually impassable. That means that the gorge will be impassable. Running it today is truly insane, but for some reason I am not afraid, and for some reason I know that today is a day that I *can* do the impossible. I can't go up there to help them or even get near enough to say good bye. Anyway, they will just try one more time to talk me out of it, and this time probably even Gandor will be on their side after the trashing that he took. I hope they'll understand, I simply must continue."

So with a final wave and a shout of "Goodbye," that she knew they could not hear, she turned away from Fidget, Gandor, Gabby, Carmine, and Sarah, and renewed her course down the Sanderson without her lifelines.

Sally was again surrounded by a peaceful silence. The river had reverted to its gentle-giant demeanor, and gave no hint of what was to come. But Sally's serenity did not last long, for as she rounded the next bend it all came back to her. This was the spot she and Gandor had seen as they flew over it in her dream, and the granite wall that was beginning to tower over her was the same granite wall that marked the beginning of the gorge. Here was the last chance she would have to change her mind, or go on as planned with her defiant, death-defying dance with the Necromancer.

As the sky darkened, the roar began, and Sally's familiarity with the scene began to fade. The atmosphere, which had suddenly become heavy, claustrophobic and foreboding, seemed to transform the growling bass sounds of the rising torrent into wrenching, demanding howls. She could see the river picking up speed as it made its turn around the granite slab, and she began to pray that she was doing the right thing. The sounds grew deafening.

"I can't wonder," she admonished herself. "Wonder creates fear, and I can't permit myself any of it! I have to focus on the next indicated thing. I *have* to get back to capturing every detail of this river in my mind's eye or my jig *will* be up!"

As Sally forced herself to concentrate on the task at hand, Amber made the final turn into the gorge. Chaos, nothing but mile after mile of it, was all an untrained eye could see, the word tumultuous falling far short to describe the violence that presented itself. Towering waves, boulders, rocks, holes, drops, and reversals all seemed to be mixed together in a continuous boiling slough. There were no gentle eddies, no quiet spots to gather one's thoughts or to plan one's moves. There was only the river's crazed attempt to remove all obstacles in its path.

"I wonder what makes you so angry," Sally said sweetly to the Necromancer as she began to mount its first giant wave.

Sally's trained eyes were able to take perfect advantage of Newton's third law of motion: For every action there is an equal and opposite reaction. Her focus was complete. What would appear to an untrained eye to be chaos was to her a dance of logical actions and reactions. Just as a world champion chess player knows many moves ahead what to expect, or a pool shark knows the final positioning of billiards after a break, Sally could see what the river was up to, what it was going to do next, and what the consequences would be for her for any given position. Time was not a factor. There was no sense of urgency. She had all the time she needed to see it all and plan it all. To her the path was as clear as a blueprint. It had to be, for any miss would lead to disaster. But she did not miss. It was as though she were a batter who could hit nothing but home runs.

H. Frank Gaertner

For the first ten miles, her canoe made its way through the river's mine fields without a scratch. Rocks, boulders, granite walls, and holes, she missed them all. Of course there was water everywhere, and at times she was even partly submerged. But Amber was prepared for that, and there was never a time Sally felt she would be tossed from the canoe. She was able to use the force of one crashing wall of water to counterbalance another, the peak of one towering wave as a launch pad for flight to a second wave, and the rising surge of a temporary backwash, as a means of escape from the depths of a collapsing hole. Mile after mile she continued her improbable death defying dance without a single misstep.

Now, however, she was faced with a seemingly insurmountable challenge, - "Phantasm Falls", - a 100-foot cascade with devastating hydraulics. There was no place for her to stop and nowhere else for her to go. Sally could see that all options were closed to her. This was the end of the road. The entrance to the portage detour that she had planned to use to by-pass the falls had been blocked during the night by a Sequoia which had given up its tenuous purchase on the gorge's cracked granite face. Her powers to "see" the river would do her no good here. All she could "see" was that she was *finished*. Fear of the Necromancer began to rise in her heart for the first time. "Is this how it is to end?" she cried.

"No! Of course not you booby!" she sharply rebuked herself. "What is it you do when you are afraid? Just let go of course! Have you forgotten that you are on a magic river, in a magic canoe, and that you are about to find what you have been seeking? Now is *not* the time to give up!" Sally went on scolding herself, as the canoe began its final approach to the 100-foot torrential drop. Abruptly she calmed her thoughts, closed her eyes, smiled peacefully, and with one sudden movement drove Amber forward and over the waiting fall with as much force as she could muster.

Chapter XXIII

THE SECRET

S he was not sure what happened. At first she fell, weightlessly, one with her canoe, for a time that seemed to her to be far too long for Phantasm's 100-foot length. But then, when she was all but convinced she had fallen into a bottomless pit, Amber hit the Sanderson with what would have been a resounding wallop had not Phantasm been drowning out all other sounds. "KA-WHAM!!! WHAM!! Wham! Wham," rang the tooth rattling crash in Sally's mind while any actual sound from the impact was made practically inaudible by the fall's incessant roar.

Momentarily sinking like a rock, Amber immediately rebounded upward like a surfacing submarine. "Holy yikes!!" Sally cried with surprise, coughing and sputtering water. "We made it Amber! We actually made it!!" Her amazed eyes were wide open now, but what greeted her did not bring her comfort, nor did it allow her to congratulate herself at the accomplishment. Obviously, the Necromancer was not yet through with her. Her successful plunge over the fall only seemed to have made the Devil's colleague all the more incensed.

Disoriented by the hard landing, Sally lost her concentration, and the chaotic scene before her began to speed up, as though someone had put a video tape into fast forward. Her mental blueprint was gone, and her ability to "see" the water and predict its course had vanished. She was at the mercy of the Necromancer, and it was as though it had just been waiting for this moment. Indeed, there could be no doubt. It was determined to show her no mercy.

An errant wave cane from nowhere. Sally was sure it was guided by the Surrogate from Hell. Having smashed her canoe into a rough slab of granite that had recently slid into the Sanderson from the wall of the gorge, a large portion of Amber's mahogany deck shattered, leaving an ugly gouge of splintered wood on the port-side bow. The jarring blow nearly threw Sally from the canoe, and *did* cause her to drop her precious paddle.

"FOCUS!!!" she demanded, and grabbed the paddle from the Necromancer's anxious grasp. "I'm sorry Amber," Sally said, acknowledging her injured craft, "I'll just have to make this up to you later. We still have work to do."

Suddenly time stopped. This was her longest freeze-frame yet, and she needed every drawn-out microsecond of it.

This is how things stood. Amber was broken, and was about to fall into a hole left by the wave that had just assaulted her. With the canoe's path already committed, all Sally could do was pray that the canoe would survive the next few moments; - moments that would be completely out of her control. Although the Necromancer had less than half a mile left to do its dirty work, she could see that it would be all she could do just to keep Amber in one piece through the rough ride ahead. As there were no more bends in the river to block her view, she could see the whole chaotic course. After that it would be smooth sailing all the way to Monarch Lake, where she hoped Fidget and the rest of the gang would be waiting.

Sally was at one and the same time excited and wary. She could not let her guard down now. Some of the most difficult rapids lay ahead. Scanning the frozen scene one last time, she committed it to memory and planned her path of escape.

"Okay. I've got it. Let's boogie Amber!" Sally urged the canoe on in a brave, challenging voice. With her focus and mental blueprint back in place Sally was ready for the last dance.

The hole swallowed her. There was nothing to do but wait and hope that the raging demon would disgorge her canoe in running condition on her predicted path. Returning from the bowels of the hole on the track of a watery conveyor belt, Amber rose to the surface with her bow heaving and cracking, and with a sound that let Sally know that it was about to break up.

"Now!" she shouted. "Paddle right!!" In a surprise move designed to leave the Necromancer guessing, Sally reversed course, and began to make her own path, as far away from the demon's planned route of destruction as she could get. Sally drew upon her experience in martial arts, shouting her surprising moves. "Ahheeee!!!" she grunted. She was on *her* path, and there was no way that the gorge's Archangel of Doom could touch her now.

On and on she paddled through the Devil's washing machine with her shouts of power echoing off the canyon walls in defiance to the Necromancer's chorus of tortured wails. Beads of sweat formed on her forehead and coalesced into rivulets that converged and poured off the end of her nose like a miniature water fall. This was by far the hardest, most difficult thing she had ever experienced, but with every stroke she knew she was that much closer to knowing the Necromancer's secret.

"The next thing, the next thing, the next thing," Sally kept repeating to herself. The mantra helped maintain Sally's detailed, intimate study of the gyrating nuances of the river's crazed attempts to unseat her. Nothing that the Necromancer threw at her worked this time. Sally anticipated all of its surprises and used its violence to satisfy her own purposes.

The final stroke to victory came unceremoniously. The Necromancer's parting shot was an anticlimactic whimper; nothing more than an ineffectual splash that even a child could have managed.

"Is that all the better you can do Neckie baby?" Sally cheered "We did it Amber!" as she whacked the surface of the Sanderson with her paddle in triumph!

Sally had accomplished the impossible. Fearless, and with a skill and finesse that even a Mohammed Ali or Wilt Chamberlain would admire, she had executed the swollen torrent with hardly a glitch. Even so, by the time Sally had cleared the gorge, and had given the Necromancer its final adieu, the only thing left holding Amber's bow in place were the flotation bags that Sally had stuffed there. But that didn't matter. They'd done it, and Amber could be fixed. She and Amber had accomplished what they had set out to do! They had defeated the Terror of the Sanderson! They had defeated the Necromancer, paddling its full length! She would see her friends again soon, and *she would at last learn the secret that the magic river held for her!*

The dark, foreboding curtain, that had been blocking the sky, separated, and a warm sun broke through the clouds to shine on Sally and Amber, chasing away the darkness that had surrounded them.

Sally was as happy as she had ever been. She had faced her worse fears and she had prevailed. In the distance she could see Monarch Lake, and on it she could see five people waving and jumping up and down on a raft that was about to capsize from the action of its over-enthusiastic occupants. She could almost hear their screams of joy.

As the river approached the lake, it had slowed to a gentle drift. A deep channel, shallow gradient, and back water from the lake, all played their role in bringing about the river's sudden change in attitude. Sally was exhausted, and the sun beating down on her was making her very uncomfortable. She urgently removed her helmet, life vest and nylon jacket, opened Amber's splash-collar and began to urge the broken canoe carefully down the slow moving stream.

Sally was looking forward to a nice lunch with her friends and a nap on the grass under a shady tree beside the lake. She would have such a story to tell her teammates, - after she had made her amends for leaving them behind. They must have been quick in rescuing the raft, carrying it to the van, and driving it to the lake in time to meet her. With the current in the gorge so swift, the trip, if you want to call it that, had only taken her about an hour. Anyway, her teammates must have hurried, because they were there to meet her, and was she ever glad to see them!

"ʀʀʀʀmmmmmtickitytickitysssshhk!!!"

"What's that!" Sally's ears perked up at the strange mixture of sounds. At first she couldn't tell what it was, only that there was a distant rumbling, sort of scrunching assortment of sounds that were growing in intensity, as whatever was causing them apparently got closer. Popping, crashing, crushing, crunching, and bashing sounds rapidly grew into torturous cries that finally combined themselves into the all-too-familiar wrenching, howling wail of the Necromancer!

"How can this be? What's going on here? This can't be happening!!" she pleaded, totally bewildered by the unwelcome surprise.

Sally was passing by one of the many unnamed creeks that emptied itself into the Sanderson. The creek meandered high up into a beautiful alpine forest that rose to her right. Looking up the creek into the forest, and in the direction of the Demonic sounds that had intensified to a deafening, murderous din, she finally saw it! The picturesque scene had abruptly transformed itself into irrational mayhem, and upon seeing it, Sally's hair actually stood on end.

"Good grief. I always thought that that 'hair-standing-on-end' stuff was a joke" she calmly mused, with a denial that was in complete contrast to the terror that was now rising in her throat.

Charging down the creek with no regard for the creek's meandering course, came an ugly, writhing, black mass, twenty feet high and one hundred feet wide. Giant Sequoias were being snapped at their base and torn from their roots. Rocks, boulders, and everything else in the path of the gruesome marauder were being devoured by it and pushed forward, as though they were subject to the action of a giant buck-scraper. The massive flash flood had been building behind a natural dirt dam that had broken its bounds due to the storm. A storm that Sally now realized must have been in cahoots with the Necromancer all along.

There was no way out. Sally just watched as the water descended upon her in a tsunami-like tidal wave filled with mud, trees, and rocks.

A troubling question forced its way into Sally's consciousness. "Is this the secret of the magic river? Is it just some kind of cruel joke?"

Brushing away the crushing defeat that the last demoralizing thought was designed to instill, Sally, determined as ever not to give up, stood up, unhesitatingly dove from her canoe with as much force as she could command, and headed for the bottom of the 25-foot depth of the channel. A powerful surge let her know that the massive black wave had arrived and had begun forcing its way into the Sanderson. Sally swam laterally downward, as fast, and as far, as she could go, hoping to miss the heavy rock debris that she knew would soon be making its way to join her at the bottom. As she swam, she made the mistake of looking up to see several large boulders coming her way.

She was about to waste precious breath by screaming underwater "Get away from me you necromancing freak!" when the river's flow increased suddenly and dramatically propelled her forward, allowing the unyielding, granite depth-charges to pass by harmlessly. The flood-swollen river continued to speed Sally away from the falling debris and headed her in the direction of Monarch Lake.

Terror upon terror filled her mind, and once more she almost made the mistake of shouting out an underwater expletive, as she visualized Amber and her teammates being consumed by the flood.

Sally had practiced and had gotten very good at holding her breath, knowing that endurance under water could come in handy in a whitewater spill. Through her diligence, she had managed to increase her capacity to two minutes. As you probably know, two minutes under water is an exceptionally long time, but by streamlining her body and using only a frog kick for propulsion, Sally was able to conserve her air, allowing her to stay down for longer than two minutes, and allowing her to escape the heavy debris. The mud was another story though. It had caught up to her and was beginning to obscure her vision. She was near the bottom of the Sanderson when a sudden urgency for air began to convulse her body. She was a long way from the surface and she finally lost it. For the first time, over the full length of her terror-filled journey, she began to panic.

"Oh God, I'm too late," she heard her inner voice cry. As Sally rose through the heavy current and ever-increasing, mud-filled turbulence, she began telling herself that she wasn't going to make it, and she began thinking that she could hear the Necromancer's gleeful cry, reinforcing her own negative thoughts.

"You're too deep! You've waited too long!" she heard it and herself wail.

"Some kind of secret this is!" Sally wise-cracked to herself with an acceptance that this could be her final, parting comment.

Looking up, and making one last effort, *she saw what looked like a person's hand reaching for her through the intensifying murky gloom.* "How can this be?" she wondered. "Who could be here, coming to my rescue?"

Confused and desperate, Sally grabbed for the hand, surrendered to its pull, and began to gulp for air.

Chapter XXIV

THE AWAKENING

J ohn Reynolds looked into his daughter's open, vacant eyes.

"It's best," he heard the doctor say to his wife, Mary.

Mary had survived the accident without injury, but she almost wished she hadn't. The decision that she and her husband were being asked to make was one that no parents should ever have to face.

Sobbing uncontrollably, Mary exclaimed with helpless, bitter rage, "It's just not right! This shouldn't be happening!"

Sally had been in a coma for more than nine months. Her attending physicians had concluded long ago that she had no hope of further recovery, that her "vegetative state" was permanent. The airbag that deployed in the accident *had* saved her body from injury, but the explosive force of the opening bag against her head damaged some critical function of her central nervous system. Exactly what had been damaged, the doctors couldn't say, but the results were obvious.

Although there was no apparent spinal cord injury, Sally had all the symptoms of a person paralyzed from the neck down. A feeding tube and a respirator were needed to keep her body alive, and except for some very active facial expressions, which coma patients often exhibit, she did not move. The doctors had concluded that it was pointless to sustain Sally's life, but the Reynolds had not been able to bring themselves to consent to what they had heard others callously refer to as "pulling the plug." Today, however, after much urging, they had finally given in.

John Reynolds hated the word "vegetative." He could not stand the thought of his daughter being characterized as a vegetable. Except for the life support system distorting her face, Sally was as beautiful as ever. Weeping, John Reynolds held Sally's hand and said "Okay, let's get on with it."

The attending nurse turned off the respirator and began to remove the tubing.

Suddenly, Sally's father felt a powerful grip from his otherwise motionless daughter, and the sound of a fearsome rattle filled the room. Sally's chest began to heave for air, and her eyes, that had moments before been lifeless, now burned with savage determination.

"Oh, I'm so sorry" the doctor reacted. "I should have *warned* you, but, given your daughter's protracted paralysis, I didn't think there was *any* possibility of this happening. It's just an involuntary response of the sympathetic nervous system. It's very common with patients in the vegetative state. Please don't be misled."

"MISLED MY FOOT!! GET HER OXYGEN - *NOW*!!! SHE'S ALIVE!!!

Chapter XXV

THE RESCUE

S ally could no longer hold her breath. She just couldn't fight it anymore. Exhausted, she began to breathe, fully expecting her lungs to fill with water. Although her initial gasps for air were as unrewarding as she expected them to be, she did not panic. Instead she relaxed, as much as is possible when one is suffocating, and began to focus on the details of her present situation. Upon doing so, she immediately noticed three things, and all of which were *very* disconcerting.

First, the hand that was pulling her to the surface felt large and familiar. "Dad?" came the odd thought. "How did you get here?"

Second, the light that was now penetrating the watery gloom of the Sanderson was harsh and seemed unnatural. It looked more like fluorescent room-lighting than sunlight, and it appeared to be shinning on the blurry image of her Mother's face.

"Mom? Are you here too?" Sally questioned. "How can that be? What happened to Fidget and the others?"

As unnerving as the first two things had been, it was the third strange thing that really got Sally's attention and accelerated her growing state of confusion.

She heard someone say "It's very common with patients in the vegetative state."

Suddenly, and coincidentally with that comment, oxygen flooded Sally's lungs and every neuron in her body seemed to fire at once.

"They think I'm a vegetable!!" she shouted to herself. Who are these people? What are they trying to do to me? What's happening here?"

Abruptly, Sally interrupted herself, noticing her rising state of panic.

"Sally, Sally," she admonished herself. "Calm down, calm down! You're letting fear take over. You are being rescued, and that's all you need to know for now. Trust in those who are helping you, relax, everything is going to be all right," she said, using her inner voice in the most soothing way possible.

As her alarm and anger dissipated, Sally got amused. "I wonder what kind of vegetable they think I am! A tomato I hope. I sure wouldn't want to be a cabbage."

The air was wonderful. It tasted delicious, forbidden, like something that she had been denied for a very long time and had been desperately craving. Breathing deeply, and trusting that she was safe, Sally reduced her intense focus and allowed herself to <u>fully</u> relax.

"Boy am I tired!" she thought. "After that ordeal all I want to do is sleep!"

Just before she closed her eyes to what was now a blinding light, Sally saw her father's face, and then knew for certain that it was his hand that had pulled her to safety. As the air had filled her lungs, she also thought she heard him shouting "She's alive!" and later, as she was drifting off to sleep, she was sure she heard her Mother crying, "Oh John! She's breathing! I can see her breathing!!"

Sally's final stream of thoughts before she fell into a deep, dreamless sleep were "Of course I'm alive," and "Of course I'm breathing! Why wouldn't I be breathing? I'm not under water anymore! What strange things for my parents to be saying. I wish I knew where I was. How did Dad get to the Sanderson? Everything is so weird. I sure hope I'm not having another dream."

Chapter XXVI

THE RECOVERY

It was very disconcerting. Sally still did not know that she had been in an accident, and that she had been comatose for nine months, nor did she know that she had slept for the last forty-eight hours.

As Sally opened her eyes, she saw her Mom and Dad anxiously smiling down on her. She tried to speak, but nothing happened. Then she tried to move, but the only thing she could do was blink and move her right hand. She was paralyzed.

As bothersome as this was, the thing that really got to her was her size. When she lifted her right arm to touch her Mom's face, she could see that she had the small hand of a young girl.

"Nuts!" she complained to herself. "This *is* a dream!"

However, any question she had about being in another dream was quickly erased when her physical therapy began. Then, there was no question she was experiencing reality, and a very painful one at that!

Slowly, Sally's memory returned. She remembered that she had been with her Mom, headed for a visit with her Grandfather. This memory came back to her when her Mom reviewed the accident one day during her physical therapy. Her mother loved to talk, and her talking helped Sally keep her mind off the pain as her body relearned how to move.

But what about her husband Fidget? She had that memory too, and it was just as vivid as any of her other memories. Not only that, she still felt like a 23-year-old woman, who badly missed her husband and her teammates, Gandor, Gabby, Sarah, and Carmine. Frequently her mother or the hospital staff would find Sally with tears welling in her eyes. No one knew why, but the psychologist said that it was a common symptom of severe traumatic-stress.

Sally needed all forms of therapy, not just the physical kind. The weekly sessions with the psychologist were helpful, but they did not start right away. She first had to spend many months with a speech therapist, relearning how to make the words that swirled in her head come out of her mouth with the appropriate sounds. The connections came slowly at first. The gargle-like noises, that she was first able to make, seemed to be totally unrelated to the word that she was trying to pronounce.

"It's hopeless," she had heard the therapist's assistant say one day, when he thought he was out of ear shot.

That comment had only stiffened Sally's resolve. Maybe they were ready to give up, but she hadn't even started.

"They just have no idea," she told herself. "I haven't gotten this far to be stopped by some silly physical limitation! I dealt with the Necromancer. I've already done the impossible. This therapy is a cake-walk by comparison!"

The gargled sounds continued to come from Sally for months. She was making no obvious signs of progress until one miraculous day the critical, missing neural connections either were somehow remade or rerouted. The therapist nearly had a stroke!

"Good morning," was all she said.

When the sessions finally started with the psychologist, Sally debated with herself whether she would share her dream experiences, but ultimately she had decided against it. The experiences were just too real and too personal. She was afraid that nobody could understand the depth of her longing to see Fidget and the others, nor, she thought, could anyone understand her flying or canoeing experiences and the importance that they held for her. Her remembrances of the dreams were vivid, and were as meaningful to her as the memory of any real-life experience. She had found the magic river, and she now knew its secret, and she now knew it had been true. She had had no choice. She had to face the Necromancer. It *had* been a matter of life and death for her, just as Gandor had said it would be.

The doctors were completely perplexed by Sally's recovery. As far as they were concerned, and as far as current medical knowledge would take them, she had been brain dead, legally deceased. Even after she started to breathe they did not expect her to recover, and even after it looked like she was going to be able to continue to breathe on her own, they did not think she would have a worthwhile quality of life. But Sally fooled them. Indeed, she fooled them all.

Sally believed that her unprecedented recovery could only be accounted for by her magic journey on the Sanderson with Amber, who, by the way, Sally was happy to learn, still hung in the family's garage - unscathed. To make sense of it all Sally devised that her dreams had been manifestations of the perilous journey she had taken through the rivers of her own mind, and that it had been the successful completion of the journey that had allowed her to make the critical neural connections needed for a return to reality.

She was also convinced that the vividness of her dreams was a key to understanding what had happened to her. Her recovery was unprecedented, and, as far as she could determine, so were her dreams. She knew, even under ordinary circumstances, that her vivid, detailed memory of these dreams was exceptional, but the circumstances were far from ordinary. Her brain, or at least the part of it that the doctors understood, could not have accommodated even the simplest thought, much less retain a memory of one. That brain had been legally dead. The doctors had concluded that the accident had triggered an area of the central nervous system that science knew little or nothing about; an area that could store memories, source dreams, command magical healing powers, and, Sally thought, just might act as the control center for paranormal ability.

The dream experiences changed Sally. She was like a different person who now approached life with new maturity and fearlessness. Although her recovery was to be long and arduous, taking almost two years to complete, she did it with grace and poise, and always with the certainty that her recovery would be total. Moreover, she did it in the face of a medical community trying their best to manage expectations of what they thought would be her limitations.

While she was recovering, Sally read a lot, most of which dealt with out-of-body, after-death, previous life, and clairvoyant experiences. But, though asked many times by her Mother, who retrieved the books for Sally from the city library, why she read such strange subject matter, she wouldn't talk about it. She would only say she found it interesting, and that the reading material was helping her rebuild lost vocabulary. In truth she hadn't lost much vocabulary, but some words did still stick in her throat. And, since her doctors encouraged her to do the reading, as part of her therapy, nobody, including her Mom, objected to her choice of subject matter. They were just glad to see that she was reading something.

Even after the miracle of Sally's re-learning how to speak, she heard one day from the head of the physical therapy department, "You've done wonderfully Sally, but don't you think you should give yourself a break? I know this is hard, but the sooner you can accept the fact that you will never be able to walk again, the sooner we can start helping you build your new life."

It certainly had looked hopeless over the many months she struggled just to move her left arm. And now that she could talk, she never stopped communicating to everyone who would listen, in the most enthusiastic way possible, just how wonderful it was going to be to do sports and learn to race Amber. Secretly, she was just waiting for the day that she would hear the head of the physical therapy department, and every other doubting Thomas say "Never mind Sally. Don't listen to us! You just keep performing your miracles!"

When it finally happened, it was just like the time she surprised the voice therapist. She had been carried to the whirlpool bath to get her ready for massage therapy. As she lay there in the swirling water, she was reminded of her struggle with the Necromancer, and of her plunge over Phantasm Falls. Vividly reliving that scene, every muscle in her body clenched with the impact of the canoe, and with the roar of the cascade rebounding off the granite walls of the gorge. *Her own sudden movements in the whirlpool bath were at least as startling to her as had been her successful dive off the 100-foot fall!*

"Holy Yikes!! I can move!!" she shouted.

When the therapist turned in response to Sally's outcry, he saw her sitting up in the whirlpool bath with her arms extended over her head like a referee signaling a touchdown. Just like the speech therapist, he became dizzy and nearly fainted. He too had become frustrated. He was sure her talk about the athletic things she planned to do was nothing but false hope, and he hated to hear her setting herself up for what could only be crushing disappointment. Once more Sally had proved them wrong.

"Take that! You necromancer freak!!" Sally shouted, slapping the water with both hands, and rejoicing at her enemy's final defeat.

Chapter XXVII

THE REUNION

S ally never said, "I told you so." The doubters were converted just as she knew they would be. She had completed her therapy and had returned to school, but there was still something that was not right with her. Sally was ten when the accident happened. She was now nearly fourteen. In her dream she had lived the life of a 23 year old woman who was in love with a 23 year old man by the name of Fred Getz. The experience had been as real as any experience can be, it had changed her life forever, but she had not wanted to share the experience with anyone. Until today, that is.

Sally had started the day like many others wondering what the dreams meant and how she could have such an experience when she was supposedly comatose. Memories of the dreams were with her constantly and she had become obsessed about getting answers to her questions regarding their meaning and origin.

As a ten year old girl, she did not have the experience or knowledge to have invented the outfitting company or the river trip. There was nothing in her past that could have given her the detailed knowledge of rafting or canoeing that she had, nor of her detailed familiarity with the white water rivers of California.

On the other hand, Sally could explain where her dream maker had gotten the idea for the valley where she met her animal friends. It reminded her a lot of the one that cradled Santa Paula, California. Her dream valley was smaller, but it had the same citrus crops that are found in Santa Paula, and the white frame house in her dream was a lot like her Grandfather's. Also, she did have some interest in canoeing and David Copperfield's magic before she had the dream, but not like now. Now she was completely hooked on both. Although, she could never see herself trying to canoe rapids like she did in the dream, she could see herself and Amber in a whitewater racing competition. As for the flying, her father had done some skydiving, and she had seen some videos of him doing it, but she had no experience of her own to draw upon. Even so, the flying had been as real for her as if she had actually done it. In fact her memory of the flying experience was just as solid as her memory of walking, swimming, or riding a bike.

Then there was the matter of Fidget, Gandor, Gabby, Carmine, and Sarah. She missed them intensely, and no matter what she did, she could not get out of her mind the idea that she had been married to Fidget. She had loved him more than life itself, and the feeling had not gone away. She felt as though her heart had broken, and until today she had seen no hope of ever fixing it.

Jerry Smith was in Sally's sixth grade, math class for gifted students. Although Jerry sat at his desk at the back of the room, quietly, doing his work, it was hard for him to keep his eyes off the long auburn hair that spread across the back of the chair six rows in front of him. He wanted to say something to the owner, but every time he got up enough nerve all he could think to say sounded really stupid. Sally, on the other hand, was oblivious. She sat near the front of the room completely focused on her work. It wasn't as though she was specifically trying to ignore anyone, but the dreams and the recovery had made her feel extremely out of place with her peers. Therefore, if it hadn't been for a dose of good old "California sunshine," it's likely that Sally would have kept to herself, withdrawing even further into a protective, isolating shell.

Los Angeles was having one of those El Nino inspired, cold, stormy days. Sally had just gotten off the school bus, and was busily trying to open her umbrella, when her algebra book slid out from under her arm. However, before she had a chance to pick the book up she heard a voice.

"May I help you?" the voice said.

He was wearing a white turtle neck sweater, brownish gray slicker, and brown leather fighter pilot's cap. Sally jumped and gasped so hard she almost swallowed her tongue. - He looked like Gandor!

"Oh, I'm so sorry. I didn't mean to startle you. My name's Jerry," he said. "I think that we are in the same math class. Here's your book."

Chapter XXVIII

THE RANCH

The road winding along a barranco, separated a eucalyptus-lined drainage ditch from adjoining orange trees. The barranco was lined with the giant trees that had been planted many years ago around the valley to protect the groves from wind. The intense perfume of orange blossoms that now filled the air brought wonderful vivid memories of the dream-valley flooding back to Sally. This was her Grandfather's ranch. It was her first visit since the fateful day more than three years earlier, and she was hopeful. Her meeting with Gandor, a.k.a. Jerry, had restored her optimism. Missing pieces of the puzzle were beginning to fall in place.

Sally kicked some clods in the road and watched the hardened, dry soil explode in dusty, chaotic clouds of dust and coagulated dirt. A surprised lizard hurried off to safety in its nearby hiding place. She loved this part of the walk which was now less than a mile from her Grandfather's home.

Earlier that morning, Sally had walked through the ranch's orange grove. She had crossed Telegraph road, and passed through one of the subdivisions that had taken over much of Santa Paula's farm land. Having come upon the large drainage pipe she was seeking, Sally had crawled through it and under the Freeway that now divided the valley, and had continued her trek onto the flood plain and bank of the Santa Clara River.

Although the river was now only a quiet stream, upon seeing it for the first time since her last visit before the accident, it reminded her of the stories she had heard from her Grandfather of the terrible day in 1928 when the St. Francis Dam broke and flooded the valley.

Sally shuddered. Suddenly she was back on the Sanderson with the Necromancer's grotesque, black wall of water and debris rushing toward her. Once again she hadn't been ready for it. The vision startled her badly, and while the memory of the nightmare no longer held any terror for her, the surprising thought was so real, she had not been sure that it wasn't some kind of omen. Consequently, Sally had turned away from the river, and quickly headed back the way she had come for home.

This day was almost identical to the one in her dream when she first met Fidget, or at least his rabbit incarnation. The sky was deep blue, the clouds were pure white, the air was warm from a slight Santa Ana breeze that blew through Sally's long, un-braided, hair, and she was in paradise. Yet, Sally continued to feel a deep longing. Even though it made her happy to believe that all of her friends, not just Gandor, would show up some day, she knew she'd never again see her animal friends. The memories of them were so dear, so special, and the loss them was so very real, that she was about to cry, when - -.

"Flap! Flap!! Flap!!! Flap!! Flap!" The large raven's wings practically brushed Sally's face. It had swooped down from one of the tall eucalyptus trees on the other side of the barranco, and it had passed right in front of Sally to land on top of a nearby orange-tree. Sally froze in place and looked at the raven for a long time for any sign of recognition. There were many of the black, large birds in the area, but this one's apparent, fearless attentiveness for Sally was decidedly unusual. After a time the raven cocked its head and winked. It then beat its wings to fly a little further down the road, and cawed repeatedly.

"Sounds just like a crow to me," said Sally somewhat disappointed, as she strained to understand what the raven was trying to say.

Just then, a large jackrabbit hopped onto the road. The rabbit stopped, looked at Sally, and hopped away in the direction of the raven, which was now positioned about 200 feet further down the road on top of an old black smudge pot. Sally began to follow after the rabbit, but before she got very far a gray squirrel ran out of the barranco toward Sally. It came to a stop about 20 feet in front of her and swished its tail at her just as she had seen Gabby do so many times.

"Oh my," Sally sighed. New tears filled her eyes, but this time not sad ones. There was just one of her friends left to find, and she would have all of her animal friends back with her again.

The coyote stood on the other side of the barranco looking at Sally walking toward the raven and rabbit. He was also eyeing the gray squirrel running ahead of Sally by just a few feet. Sally did not notice the coyote at first, but when she did, she could go no further. It was just too overwhelming. She dropped to her knees, hard. Collapsing further, she ended up sitting cross-legged with her elbows on her knees and her head in her hands in the middle of the dirt road. The raven, rabbit and squirrel saw the coyote too, but they showed no fear.

Time stood still. Nothing moved. Even the birds and insects stopped their chirping and buzzing. As the animals looked at Sally and each other, she looked back at them with loving tears and obligatory nasal discharge.

"I sure have been happy a lot lately." At that thought Sally began to laugh out loud.

Hearing her laughter the raven cawed, but still did not say anything intelligible, and flew away. Likewise, the rabbit and squirrel disappeared into the orange grove. The coyote, however, stood its ground on the other side of the barranco and continued to study Sally. She was sure that she saw it give her a broad canine grin, and then it too turned, and disappeared behind the wind-break of eucalyptus trees.

Sally stood, wiped her eyes and nose on her blue checkered shirt, and paused for a moment. "I wonder - - - ?" began the curious thought.

Without further hesitation, Sally closed her eyes, lifted her arms skyward, raised her right leg, as if she were stepping up onto an imaginary stairway, and - - -.

Sally's bedtime managerie

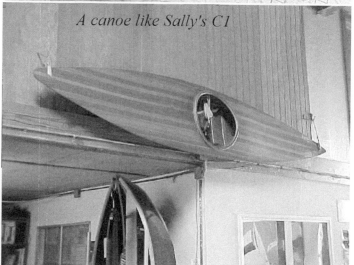

A canoe like Sally's C1

When I First wrote Sally in 1997 I had no idea that anyone would purposely launch themselves off a 100-foot waterfall. So I was quite surprised to see, sometime after I finished writing the first edition, a framed picture in a ski shop of someone actually doing such a thing. I recently found the following picture on the internet. Check out Erik Boomer's website and see him on YouTube®. You will be amazed!